THE CHRIST OF INDIA

THE CHRIST OF INDIA

The Story of Saint Thomas Christianity

ABBOT GEORGE BURKE
(SWAMI NIRMALANANDA GIRI)

LIGHT OF THE SPIRIT
PRESS
CEDAR CREST, NEW MEXICO

Published by
Light of the Spirit Press

Light of the Spirit Monastery
P. O. Box 1370
Cedar Crest, New Mexico 87008

www.OCOY.org

Copyright © 2016 Light of the Spirit Monastery.
All rights reserved.

ISBN-13: 978-1535100632
ISBN-10: 153510063X

Library of Congress Control Number: 2016911331
CreateSpace Independent Publishing Platform, North Charleston, SC

Because of the dynamic nature of the Internet, any web addresses or links contained in this book may have changed since publication and may no longer be valid.

Table of Contents

Preface..vii
The Christ of India..1
The Apostle of India..25
Basic Beliefs of Saint Thomas Christianity...........................49
The Saint Thomas Christian View of Dharma.....................75
Glossary..82
About the Author..88
More from Light of the Spirit Press.......................................89

Preface

Saint Thomas Christianity is that unique form of the teachings of Jesus of Nazareth that was established exclusively in India by Saint Thomas the Apostle. The material in this book will reveal that this statement is simple fact without exaggeration.

The best statement of the basic beliefs and attitudes of Saint Thomas Christianity is the Creed which was printed in the fourth edition of the Liturgy of the Liberal Catholic Church (which has its philosophical roots in India):

> We believe in God, the undivided Unity, embracing all in oneness.
> We believe in the Holy and all-glorious Trinity, who pervades the whole universe, who dwells also in the spirit of man.
> We believe in Jesus Christ, the Lord of love and wisdom, first among his brethren, who leads us to the glory of the Father, who is himself the way, the truth, and the life.
> We believe in the law of good which rules the world and by which one day all his sons shall reach the feet of the Father, however far they stray.
> We strive towards the ancient narrow path that leads to life eternal. So shall his blessing rest on us and peace forevermore. Amen.

Saint Thomas Christianity has two aspects: 1) philosophy and spiritual practice, and 2) ritual.

The philosophy of Saint Thomas Christianity is classical Sanatana Dharma as found in the Upanishads and the Bhagavad Gita and other spiritual writings of India. The spiritual practice of Saint Thomas Christianity is Yoga: Om Yoga specifically.

The ritual of Saint Thomas Christianity consists of worship and blessing and spiritual empowerment. These rites are known as Sacraments and Sacramentals. They were all instituted by Jesus, but the original forms were lost in passing centuries. Therefore the Saint Thomas Christians in America use the esoteric forms based on Western and Eastern Christian rituals that were formulated by Bishops Wedgwood and Leadbeater, Theosophists who were also advaitans and yogis.

As the angel said to Saint Augustine: Take and Read.

> NOTE: I wish to apologize that many quotations in this book have no attribution. Much of the material presented in the sections "The Christ of India" and "The Apostle of India" was gathered from books which I found in both North and South India, printed by the Indian Society For The Propagation of Christian Knowledge, the Roman Catholic Church and the Saint Thomas Church. I put it all in typewritten form just for my personal use, not foreseeing any other situation. Having read the books myself I never thought of the very real need for complete documentation in case one day I might want to print some or all of it.

Throughout the text are references to articles which may be found on our website, www.OCOY.org.

The Christ of India

Essene roots of Christianity

At the time of Jesus of Nazareth there were two major currents or sects within Judaism: the Pharisees and the Sadducees. The Pharisees were extremely concerned with strict external observance of their interpretation of the Mosaic Law, ritual worship, and theology. The Sadducees, on the other hand, were very little concerned with any of these and tended toward a kind of genteel agnosticism. Today these two groups might be compared with the Orthodox and the Reformed branches of Judaism respectively.

There was also a third sect which both was and was not part of Judaism. They were the Essenes, whose very name means "the Outsiders." "Essene" is the Greek equivalent of the Hebrew *Chitsonim*, "the outsiders." Since Philo and other Jewish historians used "Essene" in writing about them, that has become the common usage. Whether they chose this name for themselves or whether it was applied to them by the disdainful Pharisees and Sadducees is not known. But that they were incongruent (even incompatible) to the normal life of Israel at that time is certainly known.

Jesus of Nazareth was an Essene, as were most of his followers, including the twelve Apostles. When Jesus said "I will build my church"

(Matthew 16:18), the word used in the Greek text of the Gospels is *ecclesia*, which literally means "the called out" or "the separated" in the sense of "the aliens." It is not far-fetched, then, to wonder if the correct translation should not be: "I will establish my *Essenes*." Many elements distinguished and even separated the Essenes from the rest of Israel.

Their claim about their very existence was certainly a controversial matter. For the Essenes averred that Moses had created them as a secret fraternity within Judaism, with Aaron and his descendants at their head. The prophet Jeremiah was a Master of the Essenes, and it was in his lifetime that they ceased to be a secret society and became a public entity. From that time many of the Essenes began living in communities. Isaiah and Saint John the Baptist were also Masters of the Essenes. Their purpose was to follow a totally esoteric religious philosophy and practice that was derived from the Egyptian Mysteries. As the grandson of the Pharaoh, Moses had been an initiate of those mysteries and destined to ultimately become the head of the Egyptian religion. It was common in Egypt for the eldest son of the Pharaoh to inherit the throne, and the next eldest son to be made the head of the Egyptian religion. Although Moses was the only son of the Pharaoh's daughter, he was adopted and his bloodline was not known. For this reason he could not be Pharaoh, but he could be put into the position usually given to the second son. The Egyptian Mysteries were themselves derived from the religion of India: Sanatana Dharma, the Eternal Religion. Because of this the Essenes had always maintained some form of contact and interchange with India–a fact that galled their fellow Israelites. Regarding this, Alfred Edersheim, in his nineteenth century classic *The Life and Times of Jesus the Messiah*, wrote: "Their fundamental tendency was quite other than that of Pharisaism, and strongly tinged with Eastern elements."

The reality of this contact with India is shown in the *Zohar* (2:188a-b), a compilation of ancient Jewish mystical traditions and the major text of the Jewish Kabbalah. It contains the following incident regarding the knowledge of an illumined rabbi concerning the religion of India and the Vedic religious rite known as the sandhya, which is an offering of prayers at dawn and sunset for enlightenment.

"Rabbi Yose and Rabbi Hiyya were walking on the road. While they were walking, night fell; they sat down. While they were sitting, morning began to shine; they rose and walked on. Rabbi Hiyya said, 'See, the face of the East, how it shines! Now all the children of the East [in India], who dwell in the mountains of light [the Himalayas], are bowing down to this light, which shines on behalf of the sun before it comes forth, and they are worshipping it.… Now you might say: 'This worship is in vain!' but since ancient, primordial days they have discovered wisdom through it."

Their contact and interchange with Indian religion–Brahminical practices in particular–were manifested in several ways among the Essenes:

1. They practiced strict non-violence.

2. They were absolute vegetarians and would not touch alcohol in any form. Nor would they eat any food cooked by a non-Essene. Edersheim says: "Its adherents would have perished of hunger rather than join in the meals of the outside world."

3. They refused to wear anything of animal origin, such as leather or wool, usually making their clothes of linen.

4. They rejected animal sacrifice, insisting that the Torah had not originally ordered animal sacrifice, but that its text had been corrupted in regard to that and many other practices as well. Their assertion was certainly corroborated by passages in the scriptures such as: "Will I eat the flesh of bulls, or drink the blood of goats?" (Psalms 50:13). "To what purpose [is] the multitude of your sacrifices unto me? saith the Lord:…I delight not in the blood of bullocks, or of lambs, or of he goats" (Isaiah 1:11). "For I spake not unto your fathers, nor commanded them in the day that I brought them out of the land of Egypt, concerning burnt offerings or sacrifices" (Jeremiah 7:22). The quotation from Isaiah is particularly relevant since he was himself the Master of the Essenes.

3

It was the Essenes' contention that the "animals" originally offered in sacrifice were symbolic effigies of animals that represented the particular failing or fault from which the offerer wished to be freed. Appollonius of Tyana taught this same thing in relation to the ancient Greek sacrifices, and urged a return to that form. Long before that, in India dough effigies were offered in "sacrifice." (See page 42 of *Ganesha*, by Chitralekha Singh and Prem Nath, published by Crest Publishing House of New Delhi.) In the Essene practice, each person molded the effigies himself while praying and concentrating deeply on the traits he wished to have corrected, feeling that they were being transferred into the image. The effigies were made of five substances: powdered frankincense, flour, water, olive oil, and salt. When these had dried, they were taken to the tabernacle whose altar was a metal structure with a grating over the top and hot coals within. The effigies were laid upon this grating and burnt by the intense heat. As they burned, through the force of the heat the olive oil and frankincense liquefied and boiled or seeped upward. This fragrant liquid was called "the blood" of the sacrifice. It was this with which Moses consecrated the tabernacle, its equipment, and the priests (Exodus 24:6,8), not animal blood. And it was just such a "lamb" whose "blood" was sprinkled on the doorposts in Egypt (Exodus 12:7).

For the Passover observance, the Essenes would bake a lamb effigy using the same ingredients, except for the frankincense they would substitute honey and cinnamon. (Or, lacking honey, they would use a kind of raisin syrup.) This was the only paschal lamb acceptable to them–and therefore to Jesus and his Apostles.

Consequently, the Essenes refused to worship in Jerusalem, but maintained their own tent-tabernacle on Mount Carmel made according to the original directions given to Moses on Mount Sinai. They considered the Jerusalem temple unacceptable because it was a stone structure built in Greco-Roman style rather than the simple and humble tabernacle form given to Moses–a form that symbolized both the physical and psychic makeup of the human being. Further, the Jerusalem temple was built by Herod who, completely subservient to Rome, disdained Judaism and practiced a kind of Roman agnostic piety. Because of this the temple was ritually unclean in their estimation. They placated the Jerusalem Temple priests by sending them large donations of money. On occasion they gave useful animals to the Temple in Jerusalem, but only with the condition that they would be allowed to live out their natural span of life.

5. They interpreted the Torah and other Hebrew scriptures in an almost exclusively spiritual, symbolic and metaphysical manner, as did the Alexandrian Jewish philosopher Philo. They also had esoteric writings of their own which they would not allow non-Essenes to see. (The original Christians had the same restriction.) But even more objectionable to the other Hebrews was their study and acceptance of "alien" scriptures–the holy books of other religions–so much so that an official condemnation was made of this practice. In light of this we can say that the Essenes were perhaps the first in recorded history to hold a universal, eclectic view of religion.

6. Celibacy was prized by them, being often observed even in marriage, and many of them led monastic lives of total renunciation.

7. They considered their male and female members–all of whom were literate–to be spiritual equals, and both sexes were prophets and teachers among them. This, too, was the practice in Hinduism at that time, women also wearing the sacred thread.

8. They denied the doctrine of the physical resurrection of the dead at the end of time, which was held by the Pharisees and later became a tenet of Mediterranean Christianity.

9. They believed in reincarnation and the law of karma and the ultimate reunion of the soul with God. This is clearly indicated by the Apostles asking Jesus about a blind man: "Master, who did sin, this man, or his parents, that he was born blind?" (John 9:2. See *May a Christian Believe in Reincarnation?*).

10. They believed that the sun was a divine manifestation, imparting spiritual powers to both body and mind. They faced the rising and setting sun and recited prayers of worship, refusing upon rising in the morning to speak a single word until the conclusion of those prayers. They did not consider the sun was a god, but a symbol of the One God of Light and Life. It was, though, felt that appropriate prayers directed toward the sun would evoke a divine response. (See Jesus' words to the king of Kashmir as recorded in the *Bhavishya Maha Purana* that are given later on.)

11. They believed in both divination and the powers of prophecy.

12. They believed in the power of occult formulas, or mantras, as well as esoteric rituals, and practiced theurgy (spiritual "magic") with them.

13. They believed in astrology, cast horoscopes, and made "magical" amulets of plants and gems according to astrological aspects. They also believed that angels had taught Moses the practice of herbalism.

14. They believed that miraculous cures were natural extensions of authentic spiritual life.

15. They would wear only white clothes as a sign that they worshipped God who is Light and were clothed by him in light. This so provoked the other Israelites that praying in white clothing was prohibited by the Pharisees and Sadducees, and laws were drafted accordingly. (The Mishnah *begins* with such a prohibition.) The disciples of Saint Thomas in India had a similar rule, only wearing white clothes in worship.

16. They observed the identical rules of purity (shaucha/shuddhi) as the Brahmins in India at that time, especially in the matter of bathing frequently.

17. They practiced the strictest adherence to truthfulness. (Travelers in past centuries cited the strict adherence to truth by the Brahmins of India as a great and admirable wonder.)

It should also be noted that most of these Brahminical practices were observed by Buddhists as well. So it is not out of place to consider that the Essenes–and Jesus and his disciples–possessed the qualities of both Hindu and Buddhist religion in "the West" at that time.

From all this we can see why Edersheim states that "In respect of doctrine, life, and worship, it [the Essene community] really stood *outside* Judaism." As a result of these differences from ordinary Judaism, the Essenes lived totally apart from their fellow Hebrews, usually in separate communities or in communal houses in the towns and cities. (The supposed "communal experiment" in the book of Acts (4:32) was really a continuation of the Essene way of life. The Last Supper took place in just such an Essene "house.")

The history of Isha Messiah–Jesus the Christ

Among the Essenes of Israel at the threshold of the Christian Era, none were better known or respected than Joachim and Anna of Nazareth. Joachim was noted for his great piety, wealth, and charity. The richest man in Israel, his practice was to annually divide his wealth into three parts, giving one to the temples of Carmel and Jerusalem and one to the poor, keeping only one part for himself. Anna was renowned as a prophetess and teacher among the Essenes. Their daughter Mary [Miryam], who had been conceived miraculously beneath the Holy of Holies of the Temple, had passed thirteen years of her life as a Temple virgin until her espousal to Joseph of Nazareth. Before their marriage was performed, she was discovered to have conceived supernaturally, and in time she gave birth to a son in a cave at Bethlehem. His given name was Jesus (Joshua: Yeshua in Aramaic and Yahoshua in Hebrew).

This son of Miryam was as miraculous as his mother, and astounding wonders were worked and manifested daily in his life–for the preservation of which his parents took him into Egypt for some years where they lived with various Essene communities there. But before that flight, when the child had been about three years old, sages from India (Matthew 2:1, 2) had come to pay him homage and to establish a link of communication with him, for his destiny was to live most of his life with them in the land of Eternal Dharma before returning to Israel as a messenger of the very illumination that had originally been at the heart of the Essene order. Through the intermediary of merchants and travelers both to and from India, contact was maintained with their destined disciple.

At the age of twelve, during the passover observances on Mount Carmel (not in Jerusalem), Jesus petitioned the elders of the Essenes for initiation—something bestowed only on adults after careful instruction and scrutiny. Because of his well-known supernatural character, the elders examined him before all those present. Not only could he answer all their questions perfectly, when the examination was ended he began to examine *them*, putting to them questions and statements that were utterly beyond their comprehension. In this way he demonstrated that the Essene order had nothing whatever to teach him, and that there was no need for him to undergo any initiation or instruction from them.

Upon his return to Nazareth preparations were begun for his journeying into India to formally become a disciple of those masters who had come to him nine years before. The necessary preliminaries being completed, Jesus set forth on a spiritual pilgrimage that would end at the feet of the three masters who would transform Jesus the Nazarene into Isha the Lord, the Teacher of Dharma and Messiah of Israel. Nicholas Roerich, in his book *Himalaya: A Monograph*, said that according to the Tibetan scrolls he found in 1925, Isha was thirteen when he left for India. The *Nathanamavali* of the Nath Yogis, which we will be considering later on, says that Isha reached India when he was fourteen.

The spiritual training of Jesus

In India the masters initiated Jesus into yoga and the highest spiritual philosophy, giving him the spiritual name "Isha," which means Lord, Master, or Ruler, a descriptive title often applied to God (Ishwara). It is also a title of Shiva. For some time Jesus meditated in a cave north of the present-day city of Rishikesh, one of the most sacred locales of India.

This is the cave north of Rishikesh in which Jesus lived for some time. In the last century both Swami Rama Tirtha and Swami (Papa) Ramdas lived there (at separate times), and had visions of Jesus meditating there, though they had no prior knowledge of his having lived there.

Varanasi (Benares)

Jesus also lived for some time in Benares, the sacred city of Shiva, the formless Absolute. The worship of Shiva centered in the form of the natural elliptical stone known as the Shiva Linga (Symbol of Shiva) which was a part of the spiritual heritage of Jesus, for his ancestor Abraham, the father of the Hebrew nation, was a worshipper of that form. The Linga which he worshipped is today enshrined in Mecca within the Kaaba. The stone, which is black in color, is said to have been given to Abraham by the Archangel Gabriel, who instructed him in its worship.

Such worship did not end with Abraham, but was practiced by his grandson Jacob, as is shown in the twenty-eighth chapter of Genesis. Unwittingly, because of the dark, Jacob used a Shiva Linga for a pillow and consequently had a vision of Shiva standing above the Linga which was symbolically seen as a ladder to heaven by means of which devas (shining ones) were coming and going. Recalling the devotion of Abraham and Isaac, Shiva spoke to Jacob and blessed him to be an ancestor of the Messiah. Upon awakening, Jacob declared that God was in that place though he had not realized it. The light of dawn revealed to him that his pillow had been a Shiva Linga, so he set it upright and worshipped it by pouring oil over it, as is traditional in the worship of Shiva, naming it (not the place) Bethel: the Dwelling of God. (In another account in the thirty-fifth chapter, it is said that Jacob "poured a drink offering thereon, and he poured oil thereon." This, too, is a traditional form of worship and offering.) From thenceforth that place became a place of pilgrimage and worship of Shiva in the form of the Linga stone. Later Jacob had another vision of Shiva, Who told him: "I am the God of Bethel, where thou anointedst the pillar, and where thou vowedst a vow unto me" (Genesis 31:13). A perusal of the Old Testament will reveal that Bethel was the spiritual center for the descendants of Jacob, even above Jerusalem.

Although this tradition of Shiva [Linga] worship has faded from the memory of the Jews and Christians, in the nineteenth century it was evidenced in the life of the stigmatic Anna Catherine Emmerich, an Augustinian Roman Catholic nun. On several occasions when she was deathly ill, angelic beings brought her crystal Shiva Lingas which they had her worship by pouring water over them. When she drank that water she would be perfectly cured. Furthermore, on major Christian holy days she would have out-of-body experiences in which she would be taken to Hardwar, a city sacred to Shiva in the foothills of the Himalayas, and from there to Mount Kailash, the traditional abode of Shiva, which she said was the spiritual heart of the world. (See the two-volume *Life of Anna Katherina Emmerich* by Karl Schmoger.)

Jagannath Puri

Jesus lived for a while in Jagannath Puri, which at that time was a great center of the worship of Shiva, second only to Benares. In Puri Jesus lived some time in the famous Govardhan Math, today a major center of the monastic order of the foremost philosopher-saint of India known as Adi Shankaracharya.

In the nineteen-fifties, the former head of the Govardhan Math, and senior figure of the entire monastic Swami Order of Shankaracharya, Jagadguru Bharati Krishna Tirtha, claimed that he had discovered "incontrovertible historical evidence" that Jesus had lived in the Govardhan Math as well as in other places of India. He was writing a book on the subject, but died before it could be finished. Unfortunately the fate of his manuscript and research is presently unknown.

The guru of Paramhansa Yogananda, Swami Sri Yukteswar Giri, had an ashram in Puri and he, too, wrote a book proving that Jesus had lived in India and been a teacher of Sanatana Dharma. (Perhaps he had access to the same material the Shankaracharya later found.) A missionary asked to borrow it and never returned it. After the passing of Sri Yukteswar his disciples asked for the return of the book but the missionary denied having it.

Return to the West

During the years he lived in India Jesus visited many spiritual centers both Hindu and Buddhist, including some in Ladakh as will be seen later, then set forth on his return journey to Israel with the blessings of the masters. Jesus was aware of the form and purpose of his death from his very birth. But it was the Indian masters who made everything clear to him regarding them. They promised Jesus that he would be sent a container of Himalayan Balsam to be poured upon his head by a close disciple as a sign that his death was imminent, even "at the door." When Saint Mary Magdalene performed this action in Bethany, Jesus understood the unspoken message, saying: "She is come aforehand to anoint my body to the burying" (Mark 14:8).

All along his way, especially in Persia, Jesus taught those who were drawn to his spiritual magnetism and who sought his counsel in the divine life. Arriving in Israel, he went directly to the Jordan where his cousin John, the Master of the Essenes, was baptizing. There his Christhood was revealed to John and those who had "the eyes to see and the ears to hear" (Deuteronomy 29:4; Matthew 3:13-17). In this way his brief mission to Israel was begun. Its progress and conclusion are well known, so we need not recount it here except to rectify one point.

Misunderstanding becomes a religion

Throughout the Gospels we see that the disciples of Jesus consistently misunderstood his speaking of higher spiritual matters. When he spoke of the sword of wisdom, they showed him swords of metal to assure him they were well equipped (Luke 22:36-38). When he warned them against the "leaven" of the Scribes and Pharisees they thought he was complaining that they did not have any bread (Mark 8:15,16). Is it any wonder then, that he said to them: "Perceive ye not yet, neither understand? have ye your heart yet hardened? Having eyes, see ye not? and having ears, hear ye not? How is it that ye do not understand?" (Mark 8:17, 18, 21). Even in the moment of his final departure from them, their words showed that they still be[lieved the] kingdom of God was an earthly political entity and not th[e realm of] spirit (Acts 1:6).

This being so, the Gospels themselves must be approached with grave caution and with the awareness that Jesus was not the creator of a new religion, but a messenger of the Eternal Religion he had learned in India. As a priest of the Saint Thomas Christian Church of South India once commented to me: "You cannot understand the teachings of Jesus if you do not know the scriptures of India." And if you do know the scriptures of India you can see where–however well-intentioned they may have been–the authors of the Gospels often completely missed the point and garbled the words and ideas they heard from Jesus, even attributing to him incidents from the life of Buddha and mistaking his quotations from the Upanishads, the Bhagavad Gita and the Dhammapada for doctrines original to him. For example, the opening verse of the Gospel of John, which has been cited through the centuries as proof of the unique character and mission of Jesus, is really a paraphrase of the Vedic verse: "In the beginning was Prajapati, and with Him was the Word." (*Prajapati vai idam agra asit. Tasya vak dvitiya asit.* Krishna Yajurveda, Kathaka Samhita, 12.5, 27.1; Krishna Yajurveda, Kathakapisthala Samhita, 42.1; Jaiminiya Brahmana II, Samaveda, 2244).

Having confused Christ with Jesus, things could only go downhill for them and their followers until the true Gospel of Christ was buried beneath two millennia of confusion and theological debris. The true teachings of Jesus are to be found in their original sources, the Upanishads, the Bhagavad Gita and the Dhammapada, for he preached no new religion but the eternal truth he had learned in India. (The most accurate record of Jesus' teachings is not contemporary with him. It is *The Aquarian Gospel of Jesus the Christ* written in the beginning of the twentieth century. There his journey to India is described.)

Return to India–not ascension

It is generally supposed that at the end of his ministry in Israel Jesus ascended into heaven. But Saint Matthew and Saint John, the two Evangelists that were eye-witnesses of his departure, do not even mention such a thing, for they knew that he returned to India after departing from them. Saint Mark and Saint Luke, who were not there, simply speak of Jesus being taken up into the heavens. The truth is that he departed to India, though it is not unlikely that he did rise up and "fly" there. This form of travel is not unknown to the Himalayan yogis even today.

That Jesus did not leave the world at the age of thirty-three was written about by Saint Irenaeus of Lyon in the second century. He claimed that Jesus lived to be fifty or more years old before leaving the earth, though he also said that Jesus was crucified at the age of thirty-three. This would mean that Jesus lived twenty years after the crucifixion. This assertion of Saint Irenaeus has puzzled Christian scholars for centuries, but if we put it together with other traditions it becomes comprehensible. Basilides of Alexandria, Mani of Persia, and Julian the Emperor said that Jesus had gone to India after His crucifixion.

Why did Jesus return to India? Anna Catharine Emmerich said that in her visions of Jesus' life she clearly saw that in India Jesus loved the people and was wholeheartedly loved in return. Even more, everyone there understood everything Jesus had to say and teach. In contrast, he was little liked in Israel and virtually no one knew what he was talking about. This would certainly be an inducement to return. There may be another reason. Some contemporary anthropologists and historians believe that Abraham was a member of the Yadava clan of Western India, the family of Krishna, who disappeared from India after Krishna's departure from this world. Swami Bhaktivedanta, founder of the Hare Krishna movement, said the same. If this is so, then Jesus was really returning to the homeland of his ancestors.

And finally, Jesus may have realized that his teachings could only be preserved in the context of Eastern religion and philosophy. An ancient

Chinese text on the history of religions and their doctrines, known as *Glass Mirror*, had this to say about Lord Isha (Jesus) and His teachings: "Yesu, the teacher and founder of the religion, was born miraculously.... His doctrines did not spread extensively, but *survived only in Asia*."

Some Buddhist historical records about Jesus

A contemporary written record of the life and teachings of Jesus in India was discovered in 1887 by the Russian traveler Nicholas Notovitch during his wanderings in Ladakh. He had it translated from the Tibetan text (the original, kept in the Marbour monastery near Lhasa, was in Pali) and, despite intense opposition from Christians in Russia and Europe, published it in his book *The Unknown Life of Jesus Christ*. When in Rome presenting his findings, he was advised by two high-ranking church officials that he should not print the book. One of them, however, told him that there were manuscripts dealing with Jesus' life and study in India secreted in the Vatican library.

As would be expected, the authenticity of Notovitch's book was attacked and various articles written claiming that the monks of the Himis monastery, where Notovitch had found the manuscript, told investigators that they knew nothing of Notovitch or the text. But both Swami Abhedananda and Swami Trigunatitananda–direct disciples of Sri Ramakrishna and preachers of Vedanta in America–went at separate times to the Himis monastery. The monks there not only assured them that Notovitch had spent some time in the monastery as he claimed, they also showed them the manuscript, part of which they translated for Swami Abhedananda, who knew from having read Notovitch's book that it was indeed the same writing found in *The Unknown Life of Jesus Christ*. Subsequently, Abhedananda had the English translation of Notovitch's text printed in India where the Christian authorities had until then prohibited both its publication or its importation and sale. Immediately after the publication of the English edition of Notovitch's book, the British Government in India hired Moslems to go throughout

Ladakh and neighboring areas posing as Hindus in search of further manuscripts about Jesus in India. They were to buy the manuscripts and bring them to their employers to be destroyed. Whether this shameful ruse succeeded to any degree we have no knowledge.

Swami Trigunatitananda not only saw the manuscript in Himis, he also was shown two paintings of Jesus. One was a depiction of his conversation with the Samaritan Woman at the well. The other was of Jesus meditating in the Himalayan forest surrounded by wild beasts that were tamed by his very presence. In America the Swami described the painting to an artist who produced the following:

Later, Dr. Nicholas Roerich, the renowned scholar, philosopher, and explorer, traveled in Ladakh and also was shown the manuscript and assured by the monks that Jesus had indeed lived in several Buddhist monasteries during his "lost years." He wrote about his own viewing of the scrolls in his book *The Heart of Asia*.

In 1921 the Himis monastery was visited by Henrietta Merrick, who in her book *In the World's Attic* tells of learning about the records of Jesus' life that were kept there. She wrote: "In Leh is the legend of Jesus who is called Issa, and the Monastery at Himis holds precious documents fifteen hundred years old which tell of the days that he passed in Leh where he was joyously received and where he preached."

In 1939 Elizabeth Caspari visited the Himis monastery. The Abbot showed her some scrolls, which he allowed her to examine, saying: "These books say your Jesus was here."

Robert Ravicz, a former professor of anthropology at California State University at Northridge, visited Himis in 1975. A Ladakh physician he met there spoke of Jesus' having been there during his "lost years."

In the late 1970s Edward Noack, author of *Amidst Ice and Nomads in High Asia*, and his wife visited the Himis monastery. A monk there told him: "There are manuscripts in our library that describe the journey of Jesus to the East."

Toward the end of the twentieth century the diaries of a Moravian Missionary, Karl Marx, were discovered in which he writes of Notovitch and his finding of scrolls about "Saint Issa." Marx's diaries are kept in the Moravian Mission museum. The pages about Notovitch and the scrolls have "disappeared" and their existence is now denied in an attempt to discredit Notovitch, but before their disappearance they were photographed by a European researcher and have been made public.

Notovitch also claimed that the Vatican Library had sixty-three manuscripts from India, China, Egypt, and Arabia—all giving information about Jesus' life.

In 1812, Meer Izzut-oolah, a Persian, was sent to Ladakh and central Asia by the East India Company. Though religion was not his mission, he observed much and subsequently wrote in his book *Travels in Central Asia*: "They keep sculptured representations of departed saints, prophets and lamas in their temples for contemplation. Some of these figures are said to represent a certain prophet who is living in the heavens, which would appear to point to Jesus Christ."

When Swami Abhedananda was in the Himis monastery doing his research on the records of Jesus' life in India he was told by the abbot that Jesus had not departed from the earth at the time his apostles saw him ascend, but that he had returned to India where he lived with the Himalayan yogis for many years.

The Nathanamavali

The Bengali educator and patriot, Bipin Chandra Pal, published an autobiographical sketch in which he revealed that Vijay Krishna Goswami, a renowned saint of Bengal and a disciple of Sri Ramakrishna, told him about spending time in the Aravalli mountains with a group of extraordinary ascetic monk-yogis known as Nath Yogis. The monks spoke to him about Isha Nath, whom they looked upon as one of the great teachers of their order. When Vijay Krishna expressed interest in this venerable guru, they read out his life as recorded in one of their sacred books, the *Nathanamavali*. It was the life of him whom the Goswami knew as Jesus the Christ! Regarding the Nath Yogis' tradition, Sri Pal comments: "It is also their conjecture that Jesus Christ and this Isha Nath are one and the same person." Here is the relevant portion of the *Nathanamavali*:

"Isha Natha came to India at the age of fourteen. After this he returned to his own country and began preaching. Soon after, his brutish and materialistic countrymen conspired against him and had him crucified. After crucifixion, or perhaps even before it, Isha Natha entered samadhi by means of yoga. [Yogis often leave their bodies in samadhi, so it is not amiss to say that Jesus did indeed "die" on the cross.]

"Seeing him thus, the Jews presumed he was dead, and buried him in a tomb. At that very moment however, one of his gurus, the great Chetan Natha, happened to be in profound meditation in the lower reaches of the Himalayas, and he saw in a vision the tortures which Isha Natha was undergoing. He therefore made his body lighter than air and passed over to the land of Israel.

"The day of his arrival was marked with thunder and lightning, for the gods were angry with the Jews, and the whole world trembled. When Chetan Natha arrived, he took the body of Isha Natha from the tomb, woke him from his samadhi, and later led him off to the sacred land of the Aryans. Isha Natha then established an ashram in the lower regions of the Himalayas and he established the cult of the lingam there." "The cult of the lingam" refers to the Shaivite branch of Hinduism. We will speak more on that later.

This assertion is supported by two relics of Jesus which are presently found in Kashmir. One is his staff, which is kept in the monastery of Aish-Muqan and is made accessible to the public in times of public catastrophe such as floods or epidemics. The other is the Stone of Moses–a Shiva linga that had belonged to Moses and which Jesus brought to Kashmir. This linga is kept in the Shiva temple at Bijbehara in Kashmir. One hundred and eight pounds in weight, if eleven people put one finger on the stone and recite the bija mantra "Ka" over and over, it will rise three feet or so into the air and remain suspended as long as the recitation continues. "Shiva" means one who is auspicious and gives blessings and happiness. In ancient Sanskrit the word *ka* means to please and to satisfy–that which Shiva does for His worshippers.

I have met two people who have "raised the Stone of Moses." One of them said that the number required to raise the stone relates to their spiritual development, and that he had raised it with only three others.

The Bhavishya Maha Purana

One ancient book of Kashmiri history, the *Bhavishya Maha Purana*, gives the following account of the meeting of a king of Kashmir with Jesus sometime after the middle of the first century:

"When the king of the Sakas came to the Himalayas, he saw a dignified person of golden complexion wearing a long white robe. Astonished to see this foreigner, he asked, 'Who are you?' The dignified person replied in a pleasant manner: 'Know me as Son of God [Isha Putram], or Born of a Virgin [Kumarigarbhasangbhawam]. Being given to truth and penances, I preached the Dharma to the mlecchas....O King, I hail from a land far away, where there is no truth, and evil knows no limits. I appeared in the country of the mlecchas as Isha Masiha [Jesus Messiah] and I suffered at their hands. For I said unto them, "'Remove all mental and bodily impurities. Remember the Name of our Lord God. Meditate upon Him Whose abode is in the center of the sun.'" There in the land of mleccha darkness, I taught love, truth, and purity of heart. I asked human beings to serve the Lord. But I suffered at the hands of the wicked and the guilty. In truth, O King, all power rests with the Lord, Who is in the center of the sun. And the elements, and the cosmos, and the sun, and God Himself, are forever. Perfect, pure, and blissful, God is always in my heart. Thus my Name has been established as Isha Masiha.' After having heard the pious words from the lips of this distinguished person, the king felt peaceful, made obeisance to him, and returned" (*Bhavishya Maha Purana* 3.2.9-31. The word *mleccha* means a foreigner, a non-Indian.)

Another Kashmiri history, the *Rajatarangini*, written in 1148 A.D., says that a great saint named Issana lived at Issabar on the bank of Dal Lake and had many disciples, one of which he raised from the dead.

When teaching in Israel, Jesus told the people: "Other sheep I have, which are not of this fold" (John 10:16), speaking of his Eastern disciples. For when Jesus came to the Jordan at the beginning of his ministry, he had spent more years of his life in India than in Israel. And he returned there for the remainder of his life, because he was a spiritual son of India: the Christ of India, messenger to the West.

Swami Sivananda

As Swami Sivananda of Rishikesh wrote in *Lives of Saints*: "[Lord Jesus] disappeared at the age of thirteen and reappeared in his thirty-first year. During this period, from his thirteenth to his thirty-first year, he came to India and practiced Yoga.…Jesus left Jerusalem and reached the land of Indus in the company of merchants. He visited Varanasi, Rajgriha and other places in India. He spent several years in Hindustan. Jesus lived like a Hindu or a Buddhist monk, a life of burning renunciation and dispassion. He assimilated the ideals, precepts and principles of Hinduism. *Christianity is modified Hinduism only*, which was suitable for those people who lived in the period of Christ. Really speaking, Jesus was a child of the soil of India only. That is the reason why there is so much of similarity between his teachings and the teachings of Hinduism and Buddhism. During [this period] he travelled in India where he got initiation from sages and seers."

And in his essay simply titled "Christianity" he also wrote:

"Christian faith sprung from the wisdom of India overspread the old trunk of Judaism. Buddhism prevailed in Palestine when Christ was born. Christ himself came in contact with it through John the Baptist. There is a striking resemblance between Buddhism and Christianity in their precepts, in their forms and ceremonies, in the architectural style of their temples, and even in the account of the lives of their founders.

"…Christianity owes to Buddhism that higher morality which distinguishes it from Judaism. The moral precepts and teachings of Buddhism have much in common with those of Christianity.

"Between his thirteenth and thirty-second years of age, Jesus spent his life in India and lived like a Hindu or Buddhist monk. He had burning Vairagya (dispassion) and spirit of renunciation. In India he assimilated Hindu ideals and principles.

"His words have been misunderstood, wrongly annotated, mutilated, deformed and transformed and yet they have survived almost two thousand years as they were very powerful and came from the heart of a realized Yogi.

"Here is the gist of Jesus' teachings: God is Spirit. He is omnipresent. He loves His creatures with infinite love. He is the Father of all. God is immanent in the world. He is transcendental also. He sent His son Jesus Christ unto the world to show them the way to attain immortality."

Satya Sai Baba

In a public talk printed in January of 1978 in *Sanatana Sarati*, Sri Satya Sai Baba spoke of Jesus' spiritual aspirations in Israel, and said: "Here [in India], his stay in the Himalayan monasteries, in Kashmir and other centres of eastern asceticism and philosophical enquiry brought him greater success. From the attitude of being a messenger of God, he declared that he was the Son of God, after returning from the East." He also stated: "In the Tibetan manuscript at the monastery where Isha spent some years the name is written as Issa. The name Isha means 'the Lord of all living beings.' Jesus proclaimed that he was a messenger of God, he wanted to emphasize that everyone is a messenger of God and has to speak, act and think as one. This is the true *karma kanda* of the Vedas, the spiritual discipline of work, of repetition of the name of the Lord, of meditation, of service."

The doubting of the Apostle Thomas

The Apostle of India

Master and disciple

In India it is often said that "the father is born again in the son." This ancient adage applies also to the worthy disciple–in him the master continues his work. This being so, the character and mission of Jesus the Christ of India can be traced in that of his apostle Thomas. Thomas is a nickname derived from the Syriac (Aramaic) word *t'omo*, which means "twin." The apostle's true name was Judas, as is recorded in the ancient Syriac gospel texts, but it was not used in later gospel texts so he would neither bear the name of the Betrayer nor be mistakenly identified with him by those who would read or hear them read.

Saint Thomas the apostle in India

After the departure of Jesus from Israel and the empowerment bestowed on his apostles at Pentecost, it was decided that they should separate and go throughout the Mediterranean regions teaching those who sought the revelation of their own Christhood (which is what "Christianity" literally means). Accordingly, eleven of the twelve apostles and many of the seventy (Luke 10:1) determined through divination where they should go and preach the Good News of Christ.

One alone did not participate in this, and that was Judas Thomas, the Twin. His assignment had been given him by Jesus himself. Thomas was to depart for India where he would live in the Himalayas with Jesus and those great masters who had taught Jesus before him. This was because Jesus had destined him for a work completely unlike that of the other apostles. He was to become the spiritual twin of his master, perhaps the most true in his likeness to Jesus both inwardly and outwardly. (It is a matter of record that Judas Thomas was also physically identical to Jesus. This was unusual but not impossible or even unknown, since he was a cousin of Jesus, as were most of the apostles.)

In the forty days between his resurrection and his leaving Israel Jesus had fully outlined to the apostles and disciples how they should teach others who would also spiritually be his disciples through them. But in India Thomas was to teach and follow another form of the Christ Way. (This is not to imply that the teachings of the other apostles were not legitimate. They were simply different; but in time they became so altered as to be alien and antithetical to original Christianity.)

So overwhelming did this task seem to Saint Thomas that he tried to avoid his mission. Yet it was not long before a government official from India came to Israel to find an architect for his king, who wished a palace built by an artisan from the land of the renowned Hiram Abiff, whose construction of the temple of Solomon was known throughout the world. Jesus manifested to him in a physical body and sold Saint Thomas to the man as a slave, giving him a signed document to that effect. When confronted with this document, Saint Thomas abandoned his resistance and left for India where he did in truth follow the steps of his master and become his twin in all things.

In the life of Saint Thomas written by the Christian Gnostic Bardaisan (154-222), based on letters written by Saint Thomas, perhaps to his Persian disciples, he is referred to as: "Twin brother of Christ, apostle of the Highest who shares in the knowledge of the hidden word of Christ, recipient of his secret pronouncements." Regarding the records of Jesus' life that he found in the Himis monastery, Nicholoas Notovitch wrote this interesting remark in relation to Saint Thomas: "[The scrolls] may have actually been spoken by St. Thomas, historical sketches having been traced by his own hand or under his direction."

Return to the West

In the Himalayas Saint Thomas was reunited with Jesus until he received the inner call to return to the West for the impending departure of the Virgin Mary from this earthly life. Just as he had been separated from his brother apostles for a special mission, so he was in the final hour of the Virgin's life. For he did not reach Ephesus in time to be present at her going forth from the body, but only came there on foot the third day after her burial. As he was approaching her tomb unawares, he was astounded to see her radiant living body emerge from the stone sepulchre and ascend. Realizing that she had finished her span of life without his being present, and fearing that he would never see her divine form again, he cried out to her in anguish of heart, imploring her not to leave him desolate. Looking upon him with loving tenderness, the Virgin took from her waist the belt she habitually wore and threw it down to him with words of blessing.

Carrying the precious relic of her belt, Saint Thomas hastened into Ephesus and announced to the grieving apostles and all those gathered in the Mother's house that she, too, was risen from the dead. Whereas he had doubted the good news of Jesus' resurrection and had received proof of its reality by touching the resurrected body of his Lord, now it was Thomas who gave physical evidence that Mary, too, was "alive for evermore" (Revelation 1:18).

The holy relic in India and Syria

Saint Thomas took the Virgin Mother's belt with him to India, and there it became the most valued treasure of his disciples, whose descendants in time came to be known as Saint Thomas Christians. A few centuries ago, in times of upheaval in India, it was taken into Syria, where during subsequent troubles in that country it disappeared. About thirty years ago the head of the Syrian Jacobite Church, Patriarch Zachariah, felt an intense urge to find the belt, and began studying the ancient records concerning it. Noticing that one of the handwritten books he consulted had an unusually thick binding, he was inspired with the thought that the belt might be hidden there. Cutting it open, he found the prize, whose simple touch began to work great miracles. (Patriarch Zachariah kept two books by his bed: the Gospels and the Bhagavad Gita. Every day he read a chapter from each of them.)

Most of the belt has been returned to India and enshrined in a great church where every Saturday (the day sacred to the worship of the Mother aspect of God in Hinduism) thousands of Christians, Hindus, and Moslems gather for the sacred Eucharist (Qurbana) and prayers to the Virgin. The miracles granted are beyond number. When I visited the shrine one Saturday as the guest of its administrator, Bishop Gregorios–who preached on the subject of the concept of Mahashakti (Supreme Power: the Divine Feminine) in Hinduism, Christianity, and Islam–I witnessed this wonderful demonstration that it is worship and not theologizing that can unite the adherents of all religions in love and harmony. Bishop Gregorios also spoke of Mahashakti being the same as the Holy Spirit, and the Virgin Mary as a perfect reflection of the Holy Spirit.

To Qumran and India

Before returning to south India for the fulfillment of his commission from Jesus, Saint Thomas went to visit the Essene communities of Israel, urging that some of them come with him to India to both escape the imminent destruction by the Romans and to help him in his spiritual work. Many did so, and a company of Essenes headed by Saint Thomas arrived in South India (Kerala) in 52 A.D. These Essenes started several villages in the same area. At the end of the twentieth century those sites were excavated and many coins like those found in the Qumran caves were unearthed.

A Hindu Brahmin family near the town of Palur, Kerala, has a document of family history wherein it is written: "In the Kali year 3153 [52 A.D.] the foreigner Thomas [Toma] Sannyasi came to our village and preached there." It is noteworthy that Saint Thomas is described as a Hindu monk (sannyasi), which he would have to have been if he truly followed in the steps of Jesus.

Ancient records say that frequently Jesus was seen in South India and mistaken for Saint Thomas. He and Saint Thomas were sometimes seen speaking together. Apparently Jesus occasionally came down from his Himalayan abode to visit Saint Thomas and supervise his work.

Jesus: Isha

Although Jesus' Aramaic name was Yeshua, since in India he was known as "Isha" (the Lord), the disciples of Saint Thomas preferred to be called Ishannis, "of Isha" (just as Lutheran means "of Luther"). Some Indian scholars such as Swami Abhedananda make the conjecture that either Ishanni is actually a derivation of Essene (Essenees), or that the Essenes themselves were called Ishannis, "Isha" in their case being a reference to Ishwara, God "the Lord." This would certainly reveal their Indian spiritual roots. However, since in time they came to refer to themselves as disciples of Saint Thomas, "Saint Thomas Christians," I will use that appellation in this study.

In his commentary on the gospels, *The Second Coming of Christ*, Paramhansa Yogananda wrote: "It is important to note the difference between Jesus the man and Jesus the Christ. Jesus was the name of the man. The Sanskrit origin of this name is found in the word 'Isha,' or Lord of Creation. Mispronounced by travelers in many lands, and being used in many different languages, the word 'Jesus' came to be used in place of Isha." This very sentiment was spoken long before by Saint Thomas himself. According to *The Acts of Thomas*, when King Mazdai, who would eventually have him martyred, asked Saint Thomas: "Who is your master? And what is his name?" Saint Thomas answered: "The name that is given to him is Jesus the Messiah"–that is, Jesus Christ (Yeshua Messiah). After the death of Saint Thomas his murderer, King Mazdai, became converted to Saint Thomas Christianity.

The disciples of Saint Thomas

Nearly all those who accepted the teachings of Saint Thomas were devout Brahmins of the highest level (Nambudiri and Nair–many of them who had emigrated from Kashmir to Kerala) who continued their religious observances, adding those that were distinctive to the Saint Thomas Christians. Acknowledging this fact, Cardinal Eugene Tisserant wrote in *Eastern Christianity in India*: "Christianity was introduced in Malabar [Kerala] and accepted spontaneously without changing the indigenous character of the inhabitants." So strict and correct were the Saint Thomas Christians in their Brahminical character and observance that they were frequently asked by the other Hindus to perform the rites of purification (*shuddhi karanam*) for defiled objects and even of Hindu temples. Today some Saint Thomas Christians still wear the sacred thread (*yajnopavita*) that is the distinctive mark of Hindu Brahmins.

Naassenes

Ancient Indian historical records sometimes refer to the Saint Thomas Christians as Naassenes. This may be a corruption of "Essene" but in the ancient Gnostic Christian texts discovered at Nag Hammadi, Egypt, we find the term "Nazoreans," so the Saint Thomas Christians may also have used it in referring to themselves. If so, this would indicate their esoteric Christian character and affinity with those esoteric Christians of Egypt–most of whom were Essenes or descendants of Essenes. Regarding the Essenes, Alfred Edersheim, in his nineteenth century classic *The Life and Times of Jesus the Messiah*, wrote: "The general movement had passed beyond the bounds of Judaism, and appeared in some forms of the Gnostic heresy."

Because of the great number of Saint Thomas Christians in the southernmost state of Kerala, it is sometimes called "the country of the Nazaranis" even today. The daily train from Madras to Kerala is known as "the Nazarani Express." When the Pope of Rome wrote a letter to the Saint Thomas Christians in the fourteenth century he addressed them as "the Nazarani Christians." Considering the spiritual character of the Saint Thomas Christians this expression could mean that they were "Nazarenes"–followers of Jesus of Nazareth. Whatever the derivation, this was definitely a name sometimes used in reference to themselves. In the Book of Acts it is said of Saint Paul by his accusers that he was "a ringleader of the sect of the Nazarenes" (Acts 24:5).

The Saint Thomas Christians had much in common with both Hindus and Buddhists. In fact, Tamil historical records contemporaneous with Saint Thomas say that he taught "a Buddhist religion." This was no doubt because of Saint Thomas' intense monastic and philosophic nature which contrasted with the usual form of Hinduism at that time, which consisted mostly of external rituals and the use of religion to attain utterly materialistic goals (*karma khanda*).

Surya Vamsa

"Surya Vamsa" was never used by the Saint Thomas Christians in speaking of themselves, but was current for centuries among the other Hindus in referring to them, and was even used on occasion in major legal documents. Surya Vamsa means "People of the Sun," Surya being a Sanskrit word for the sun. They were also sometimes called by others Suryan or Suryani. These have been assumed to mean "Syrian" because of their ties with the Syriac (Aramaic)-speaking Christians of the Middle East. But they may really be derivations from Surya Vamsa.

The Saint Thomas Christian Sampradaya

A sampradaya is a lineage of spiritual teaching stemming from an enlightened teacher, such as the Shankara Sampradaya, Ramanuja

Sampradaya, Madhavacharya Sampradaya, or according to the form of God they particularly worship such as the Shaivite, Vaishnava, Shakta, or Ganapatya sampradayas. Whatever distinctive customs a sampradaya might possess, they all consider themselves to be fundamentally followers of Sanatana Dharma, the religion based on the Vedas and the teachings of the vedic seers known as rishis. And the majority of their customs and spiritual doctrines are absolutely identical and harmonious with one another.

Even though they would have primarily described themselves as Saint Thomas Christians, they considered themselves a sampradaya within Sanatana Dharma, not a separate religion. It is historical fact that externally the Saint Thomas Christians were an integral part of Hindu society in every way. This is the trait that most horrified and infuriated the Christians from outside when they encountered the Saint Thomas Christians.

"Christians" with a difference

After their encounters with European Christians the Saint Thomas Christians began to call themselves by that name to make their spiritual nature comprehensible to them and also to affirm that their form of the teachings of Jesus was their heritage from the apostle Thomas himself and was positively to be distinguished from the Petrine (Roman Catholic) or Pauline (Eastern Orthodox or Protestant) forms of Christianity.

Although they had friendly interchange with the Eastern Christians of Persia, Syria and Iraq, they were insistent upon their distinction from them as well. Bar-Hebraeus, an early Syrian Christian writer, records that when Christians from Persia visited India the Saint Thomas Christians told them: "We are the disciples of Saint Thomas." It was those Persians who created the phrase "Saint Thomas Christians" and first began to use it.

Because there were profound ties between India and Persia–many Persians being followers of Vedic religion–the Saint Thomas Christians always considered themselves brethren of the Persian Christians, who were of the Chaldean tradition which after the destruction of Christianity in Persia became centered in Iraq. Both the Persian and Iraqi Christians were condemned as heretics by the other churches of East and West since they did not believe that Jesus Christ was God in the sense of being an incarnation of one Person of the Trinity. Rather, they believed that he had begun as a man just like us and had attained the status of Christ–Son of God–as could (and should) all Christians.

The Saint Thomas Christians believed this as well, and they, too, were called heretics by the Western Christians who persecuted them. Just as modern Christians ignore the fact that reincarnation is an orthodox Jewish belief (see *May a Christian Believe in Reincarnation?*), so they ignore that there exist two churches–one founded by the apostle Thomas in India and the other founded by the apostle Thaddeus in Iraq–with a continuous history from the apostolic age that do not believe in the Mediterranean doctrine of Jesus being the incarnation of the Second Person of the Trinity. This is why Cardinal Tisserant could (uncomprehendingly) write: "It does not seem, however, that the Indian Christians were ever greatly concerned with the great Christological disputes of bygone days." That was because the doctrinal controversies, alterations, and aberrations of Mediterranean Christianity meant nothing to them as followers of Jesus and Saint Thomas.

The fact that the Saint Thomas Christians did not originally use the expression "Christian" underscores their fundamental difference from the Mediterranean Christianity derived from the other apostles. In the last century or so, mostly as a result of pressure from the latterly mentioned Christians of the East, for the sake of expedience the titles of "Indian Orthodox Christians," "Indian Orthodox Church" and "Malankara Orthodox Church" have also become current usage.

Regarding this, Father Jacob Kurian, teacher of theology at the Kottayam seminary in Kerala, had this to say to Christine Chaillot, the author of *The Malankara Orthodox Church*: "We should feel that we have an

Indian role to play and we should present to the world a specific picture of our church. We cherish so much the Indian Orthodox Christian tradition that we could build our Christian tradition on the foundations of the *Sanatana Dharma,* that is the ancient Hindu *samskara* (ritual) life style. Of course, there is the foundation laid by Christ and the apostles and the long spiritual tradition of Christianity. But the theological tradition of the Indian Church has to be in line with the Indian philosophical tradition, which is not necessarily only the Hindu one, but also that of the Buddhists, the Jains and other non-Christian traditions which also contribute to the Indian philosophical tradition. So we have to take this into consideration together with the Eastern Orthodox spirituality and theology. We want to present to the world a model of Christianity that has lived for the last twenty centuries in a tradition of pluralism, but at the same time we want to keep the central elements of Orthodox Christian spirituality and doctrinal integrity.... When Christians adopt this attitude of *Sanatana Dharma* which incorporates all truth, they will be able to overcome all anxiety regarding syncretism"–an anxiety not on the part of the Saint Thomas Christians but on the part of those who simply do not understand their historical and spiritual character any more than they understand the true historical and spiritual character of Jesus himself, whose teachings contain quotations from the Vedas, the Upanishads, the Bhagavad Gita, and the Dhammapada.

The witness of history

History itself demonstrates the character of Saint Thomas Christianity as a sampradaya within Hindu religion.

When, because of the movement of population, the Saint Thomas Christian temples became Hindu temples, the Saint Thomas Christian icons remained in those temples and were worshipped by the Hindus along with the other images. Even more revealing was the discovery in 1925 and 1926 of scores of ancient stones at Kodiveri upon which are engraved symbols of the various Hindu sampradayas, including those of the Saint Thomas Christians. (At Tangste, in Ladakh, there are also large stone boulders upon which crosses have been carved.) It is a matter of historical record (sometimes by European Christians who were displeased) that as a matter of course the other Hindus contributed money and labor for the building of Saint Thomas Christian temples and the Saint Thomas Christians did the same when other types of Hindu temples were built. This was because they were of one religion.

The traditions of the Saint Thomas Christians say that Saint Thomas built a temple in Nilackal, presently a completely deserted area. Recent excavations in the area of Nilackal have revealed that a kind of Hindu temple city existed there at the time of Saint Thomas and that the Saint Thomas Christian temple had been built within the compound of the Mahadeva (Shiva) temple as a subsidiary temple. This demonstrates that Saint Thomas and his followers were considered a Shaivite sampradaya. At the time of Jesus and Saint Thomas, Shaivism in South India was fundamentally a philosophy of non-dualism (advaita) and yoga. Many Saint Thomas Christians still wear rudraksha beads, a mark of Shaivites.

In 345 A.D., when the ruler of Carnellur gave the suburb of Muziris to the Saint Thomas Christians for their exclusive use, they renamed it Mahadevar Pattanam, the City of Mahadeva (Shiva). The king, a Hindu, laid the first brick for the Saint Thomas Christian temple that was built there, and upon its completion he led the first service of prayers to be conducted there. This would not have been done if the Saint Thomas Christians were not themselves considered part of Hinduism. Eventually a Saint Thomas Christian kingdom, with Mahadevar Pattanam as its capital, was established. At Nilamperur, near the site of a Hindu temple, the effigy of a king wearing a pectoral cross was unearthed at the end of the nineteenth century. In the north, in the area traditionally known as the Hindu Kush, a coin from the first century was found depicting the local raja riding a horse and carrying a cross in his hand. In time the Saint Thomas Christians were made the legal patrons and supervisors of all carpenters, metal smelters, blacksmiths, goldsmiths, and barbers—whatever their religion.

Whenever a child reached the age of three years the Saint Thomas Christians always had a Brahmin pandit come to their home and symbolically begin his formal education by guiding the child's fingers to trace the mantra *Om Sri Ganapataye Namah*—"I bow to Lord Ganesha"—in a plate of rice before which a ghee lamp was burning that had previously been worshipped as an emblem of the goddess Saraswati, the goddess of wisdom and learning. This is still the custom among the Saint Thomas Christians, but the mantra is now usually *Hari Sri Ganapataye Namah*. Ganesha is the Hindu deity that is depicted with the head of an elephant. He is always worshipped before any undertaking, including, in this instance, the beginning of education. Hari is a name of the god Vishnu, the Preserver in the Hindu Trinity of Brahma, Vishnu, and Shiva. It is interesting that many of the very old Saint Thomas Christian temples in South India have golden "dharma towers" in front of them just like those in the temples of Vishnu.

In *The Orthodox Church of India* the author, David Daniel, himself a Saint Thomas Christian, writes: "The festivals in Hindu temples and Christian Churches are often festivals of the entire village community. A church procession, for example, will have the same familiar music played in Hindu temples, the same type of lace silken umbrellas, flags and festoon, decorated elephants and ear-breaking beating of drums and noise of crackers. The festivals invariably end with remarkable displays of fireworks in the night." And he concludes, "Needless to say, the Saint Thomas Christians have assimilated many of the social customs and practices of the land *and are indistinguishable as an entity in the society."*

History of the Saint Thomas Christians

In Mylapore near modern Madras, the apostle Thomas was pierced with a lance on December 19, 72 A.D., but did not die until December 21. He was buried nearby, and the earth from his tomb worked many miracles. In 1292 Marco Polo visited his tomb and took some of the red-colored earth from there. Upon his return to Venice he healed many people with it according to his own testimony.

The spiritual family of Saint Thomas continued and grew. Just before his martyrdom, King Mazdai said to him: "I have not been in haste to destroy you, but have had patience with you; and you have added to your deeds, and your sorceries are spoken of through the whole country. But I will do unto you so that they shall accompany you and go along with you [in death], and that our country shall be relieved of them." To this Saint Thomas answered: "These 'sorceries,' which you say shall accompany me, *shall never fail from this place.*" And so it has been seen to be. Saint Thomas Christianity spread throughout India, though never of large numbers. It is remarkable, but historical records indicate that there was no region of India in which the Saint Thomas Christians were not represented, though they were mostly in South India. In 1430, Nicholas di Condi in writing of his travels in India said that the Saint Thomas Christians "are scattered over India like the Jews with us." Except for the vicissitudes that all societies endure, the Saint Thomas Christians lived in complete peace, enjoying spiritual interchange with various Eastern Christian churches, though jealously maintaining their autonomy and distinctive ways.

"Christian" treachery and persecution

More than one unsuccessful attempt was made in the early centuries by the Mediterranean Christians to establish their form of Christianity in India. At the coming of the Europeans in large numbers, however, this began to change, culminating in a full-scale persecution by the Portuguese colonialists, who first came to India in 1498. Christians from Europe were always received in total friendship by the Christians of Saint Thomas and often given places to live. In many instances the Saint Thomas Christians interceded with the local rulers in gaining residency and trade permissions for the Europeans. But sadly, on the part of the opportunistic Europeans there was no such sincere openness, and as soon as any political ascendancy was attained, pressure would be brought to bear on the Saint Thomas Christians to convert to the Christianity of the Westerners.

This came to an appalling climax in the last year of the sixteenth century when the Portuguese Roman Catholic Archbishop of Goa, Alexius Menezes, summoned all the Saint Thomas Christian clergy and a considerable number of laymen to the town of Diamper to supposedly bring peace and reconciliation between the two churches. In response one hundred fifty-three priests and about six hundred and sixty laymen attended. The Saint Thomas Christians were asked to bring all their liturgical and theological texts–especially their ancient texts containing the teachings of Saint Thomas–so they could be "examined." Believing that the Europeans wanted to sincerely discover the apostolic traditions of Saint Thomas, and therefore of Jesus, they did so. Their horror was boundless when they found themselves surrounded by Portuguese soldiers who forced them at gunpoint to surrender their precious manuscripts, which were then burned in their presence at the order of the Archbishop. Because of this "It is not possible to write a complete history of the Christians in South-West India, because the ancient documents of their churches were destroyed by fire at the Synod of Diamper in 1599," as Cardinal Tisserant admits.

"What history will not willingly forgive is the literary holocaust which was carried out on the authority of this decree, when all books that could be laid hands on were consigned to the flames. It was comparable in many ways with the vandalism of Omar, who by similar wanton destruction ordered the noble library of Alexandria to be consumed by flames. The Syrian Christians of today believe that because of this cruel decree, no records are available with them to recover and establish beyond all dispute their past Church history. None will deny that there is some substance in this belief" (S. G. Pothen, *The Syrian Christians of Kerala*).

Among the books burned were many copies of three books. Two of them, *The Book of Charms* and *The Ring of Solomon*, were books of Christian magic. The third was a book on esoteric healing and the making of amulets from gems and herbs (as the Essenes had also done) called *The Medicine of the Persians*. They now exist only as nearly-forgotten names.

Not only were the books brought to Diamper destroyed, Archbishop Menezes went from church to church searching for more books and burning entire libraries in many places—even in areas where the Portuguese had no political power whatsoever. The liturgical texts containing the rites of the Chaldean tradition were especially sought out and destroyed because they revealed how utterly the other churches had departed from the original ways of Christianity, and because they expressed the correct view of Jesus as a Son of God by attainment and not as the creator God incarnate. A list of forbidden books was made at Diamper, and any who read or listened to them being read were automatically condemned.

Over the course of the next days the Archbishop also engaged in harangues to "correct" the ways of the Saint Thomas Christians and bring them into conformity with those of "the one, holy, catholic, and apostolic See of Rome." The Portuguese even forced the Christians of Saint Thomas to change the way they made the Sign of the Cross (right to left) to the way the Western Christians had only recently themselves come to do it (left to right).

Condemnations

The official acts of the Synod particularly inveighed against the Saint Thomas Christians who taught school and made provisions for the religious instruction of the students in their own religions, keeping the images of Hindu deities in the schools so the students could learn and perform their daily worship. Those who sent their children to schools taught by Hindus where they, too, worshipped the deities, were declared excommunicated (from a church to which they did not even belong!) and the children were forbidden to enter a Portuguese-established church.

Since participation in "idolatrous" worship and the making of offerings in Hindu temples was the norm for the Saint Thomas Christians—since they were a Hindu sampradaya—that, too, was soundly castigated. Especially denounced was the use of Hindu rites of exorcism by the Saint Thomas Christian priests, as well as other "idolatrous" and "superstitious" Vedic rituals. Priests who dared to have themselves registered as Nair Brahmins were condemned, not for a religious reason, but because it supposedly made them liable to be called up for military service.

Saint Thomas had given the Saint Thomas Christians a book which they used for divination to obtain guidance in the making of important decisions and to determine the future. This was a special target of the Portuguese, who also railed against the use of Hindu diviners by the Saint Thomas Christians, and all copies of this invaluable document were consigned to the flames of bigotry. However the Saint Thomas Christians still use divination of various sorts.

The Saint Thomas Christians considered astrology a legitimate means of forecast and guidance, and used it accordingly. Their priests were considered to be especially skilled in determining astrologically what days and times were the most favorable for marriage and the starting of journeys or any other type of endeavor. In David Daniel's book *The Orthodox Church of India*, published and sold by the Orthodox Church in India, we find this: "The Saint Thomas Christians are accustomed to consult astrologers to ascertain the auspicious moment for setting out for any purpose, e.g., for a journey, a wedding, etc. Drawing horoscopes is not uncommon amongst them." Many Saint Thomas Christian priests are astrologers and considered specialists in determining fortunate or auspicious times.

Oddly, condemnation was even pronounced against the Saint Thomas Christians' laudable custom of adopting as many orphans as they could so they would not be homeless. This was a custom they had inherited from the Essenes.

As it is the Hindu custom to name children after deities, the Saint Thomas Christians naturally were accustomed to sometimes name their male children Isha or Yeshua (Joshua/Jesus). This–along with their habit of giving Old Testament names, as well–was violently censured by the Portuguese.

They were also condemned for piercing their ears and taking too many baths in a day.

The Synod of Diamper did have one positive effect, though a backhanded one. By reading the fulminations against the "pagan" ways of the Saint Thomas Christians and the official condemnations of them we are able to establish that the Saint Thomas Christians were indeed practicing Hindu Brahmins who revered Jesus but considered the other segments of Hinduism–as well as the other religions of the world–to be equally viable in the search for God.

The aftermath

Hardly any of the Saint Thomas Christians could even understand the language in which all this was done, and they were forced through cajolery and threats to sign documents of concurrence with all that had taken place–these documents being represented to them as nothing more than statements that they had been present at the gathering. Before sending those documents to Rome, Archbishop Menezes interpolated many items into the signed documents to make it appear that the Saint Thomas Christians had agreed to things either not actually spoken about or that were firmly resisted by them when they were brought up.

Finally, "approved" Syriac liturgical texts were issued to the clergy along with other written directives, and they departed in a daze to their flocks, accompanied by Portuguese "assistants" who were to make sure that they carried out the demands of the Europeans.

When the Jesuits that were present at the Diamper assembly officially objected to the outrageous actions of Archbishop Menezes, he coolly remarked that "he behaved like that just to show the way of salvation to the assembled without hindrance." Cardinal Eugene Tisserant was apparently of the same mentality when, in 1957, he wrote in *Eastern Christianity in India*: "Instead of destroying the existing Syriac manuscripts, he [Archbishop Menezes] could have had them corrected, but his method was that of certainty, so that any future heresy could be more easily averted."

Thus was "the beginning of sorrows" that were to continue for nearly a century. Slowly the ways of "the faith which was once delivered unto the saints" were eroded, though in the rural and mountainous areas not prosperous enough to attract the rapacious attention of the Portuguese clerics and traders little change occurred.

The end of oppression approaches

Friendly clergy from the Syriac-speaking Orthodox Churches who came to visit their Indian brothers were arrested and deported or imprisoned. (The fact that they made no objections to the Saint Thomas Christians' obvious Hindu character indicates that in earlier centuries they themselves held comparable or compatible ideas or else considered them neither heretical nor of any spiritual detriment.) Some were actually taken to Portugal and Rome and subjected to interrogation by the Inquisition. A few were burned to death for heresy. Others vanished forever. Atrocities committed against the Indian Christians were not unknown, though never officially sanctioned by the invaders–a common tactic of tyrants.

In 1653, at the order of Portuguese ecclesiastics, a Syrian bishop (some say he was the Patriarch of the Syrian Church) who had come to find out why communication with the Saint Thomas Christians had been so long in abeyance, was imprisoned. When the Saint Thomas Christians learned of this outrage they came in thousands to protest. The bishop was then smuggled out of the prison and eventually murdered by drowning, his body being washed up on the coast a few days later. This so exasperated the Saint Thomas Christians that many thousands of them assembled at the church in Mattanchery and swore on the Coonan Cross the solemn vow that they would no longer have any association whatsoever with the Portuguese or their "Petrine" religion. Happily, this was successful, and the yoke of spiritual bondage was thrown off permanently. Despite skirmishes with the Europeans who were determined to re-impose their enslavement, the Saint Thomas Christians managed to keep their spiritual integrity, protected by the Hindu rulers from further persecution.

False friends

It is tragically true that false friendship is often more treacherous than open enmity, and so it proved to be in the nineteenth century when the Protestant missionaries (mostly Church of England) managed to exert great influence over the Saint Thomas Christians and bring about the abandonment of many valued traditions and beliefs. In time this form of invasion was repulsed to some degree, but not until many had forsaken the ways of their ancestors and embraced the minimal religion of the missionaries in place of Saint Thomas Christianity. In this way both Catholic and Protestant Europe managed to wreak undeniable and profound damage on the Saint Thomas Christian Church.

I saw the effects of this for myself when speaking at a church meeting in Niranam where Saint Thomas had founded the congregation. (Several examples of his woodwork–especially carvings in traditional Hindu temple style–were shown to me.) During my talk, I felt so galled by not being able to speak freely of the higher, esoteric aspects of religion that I decided to break loose and say what I pleased, and hang the consequences. At the far back many very elderly men and women were sitting, their heads bowed down in abject boredom and disinterest. But when I had spoken just a few sentences of real Christian belief, they all began looking eagerly at me, smiling, nodding, and gesturing to one another in approval. At the end they all surged forward to express their appreciation of my talk. It was evident that as children they had heard the very things I was now speaking, but it had been a long and dreary time since those truths had been publicly expressed.

Saint Gregorios of Parumala (1848-1902)

Saint Gregorios of Parumala

The crowning glory of Saint Thomas Christianity was the great bishop-saint Gregorios of Parumala, who lived in the nineteenth century. Every day in the major newspapers of Kerala strings of identical small icons of Saint Gregorios are printed, each one a thanksgiving for an answered prayer. In one city of Kerala I saw a shrine to Saint Gregorios at a bus stop with hundreds of candles burning before his icon in petition for those who had prayed there before proceeding on to work or school. The money contributed for the candles was there in an open box, but no one would think of stealing from it. It is a common sight along the roads in Kerala to see large wayside shrines with more-than-life-size icons of the saint enshrined in them.

The tomb of Saint Gregorios in Parumala is visited daily by thousands and tens of thousands of pilgrims–Hindus, Christians, and Moslems–for whom it flows miracles and blessings beyond counting. I can bear witness that the moment you enter the boundaries of the island-shrine you step into another world altogether, and that the room where he left his body is one of the most spiritually powerful places I have ever been. Fortunately I was able to meditate there for some time.

Here in America I met a remarkable yogi and Hindu scholar, Sri Nandu Menon. He told me that Saint Gregorios was the best friend of his strictly traditional Hindu Brahmin uncles, and spent a great deal of time with them in spiritual discussions. Nanduji told me that Saint Gregorios told his uncles that he considered his mission in life was to bring about the restoration of three essential teachings to the Saint Thomas Christian Church: 1) the belief in karma; 2) the belief in reincarnation; and 3) the belief that God and the individual spirit-self are one. Unfortunately it did not come about in India, but it has in some degree in America.

Saint Thomas Christianity in America

The end of the nineteenth century was distinguished by an incident whose far-reaching effects could not have been foreseen, except in the illumined consciousness of Saint Gregorios of Parumala.

Learning that in America a small group of Europeans who were originally Old Catholics and had converted to the Eastern (Russian) Orthodox Church were experiencing persecution from the same enemies that had recently been routed from the life of the Saint Thomas Church, he insisted to his astonished brethren that this little flock should be relieved of its fears by being accepted as an autonomous entity within the Saint Thomas Christian Church.

This was not an unheard-of idea, for in the fifth century some Christians from Persia immigrated to India and became an autonomous part of the Saint Thomas Christian Church. Today they consist of several large and prosperous parishes. When in Kerala on one trip I spent most of a day with their bishop, Mar Clemis. Interestingly, there is a single parish in Anchor, Kerala, that is officially an independent church within the Saint Thomas Christian Church. So the autonomy of the minuscule church in America seemed perfectly natural as well as necessary. Consequently the Saint Thomas Christian bishops supported Saint Gregorios and an autonomous segment of the Saint Thomas Christian Church was established by the consecration of a bishop for the American mission.

The little mission was never of any significant size, though heavily persecuted by the same enemies that had harassed them before becoming part of the Saint Thomas Church, and for nearly three quarters of a century it was confined to monastic foundations headed by Archbishop William Henry Francis Brothers, a nephew of the famous Roman Catholic Cardinal, John Henry Newman. The openly esoteric views of the monks (among whom was Bligh Bond, the clairvoyant discoverer of the holy sites of Glastonbury) did not appeal to the ordinary Americans of that day, and they were usually denounced as "theosophical"–which they happily were. Some of them even used the esoteric forms of traditional Roman Catholic rituals formulated for use in the Liberal Catholic Church by bishops James Ingall Wedgwood and Charles

Webster Leadbeater, major figures in the Theosophical Society. (See *The Yoga of the Sacraments*.)

In the nineteen-seventies the ranks of the tiny mission were joined by the monks of Light of the Spirit Monastery who eventually became all that is left of the tiny mission of Saint Gregorios. Having a background in Indian philosophy and yoga, they readily took up the original ways of the Saint Thomas Christians. (A small minority of the Saint Thomas Christians in India are advocating a similar complete return to tradition.)

In view of what has been written so far, it is a virtual understatement to say that Saint Thomas Christianity is a unique spiritual entity, vastly differing from what is commonly known as Christianity.

The Saint Thomas Christian Cross

BASIC BELIEFS OF SAINT THOMAS CHRISTIANITY

Before embarking on an outline of the various beliefs held by Saint Thomas Christians, it should be made clear that the teachings of Saint Thomas Christianity are not a set of imposed dogmas, but rather a way of spiritual life. Saint Thomas Christians emphasize *spiritual practice* and the experience and knowledge gained from such practice rather than the intellectual concepts of theology and dogma. Naturally there is a broad framework within which the Saint Thomas Christians pursue their spiritual life, but theological details are left up to the individual. Obviously a person who does not believe in God and in the spiritual legacy of Jesus and the Apostle Thomas would not become or remain a Saint Thomas Christian. Yet there are certain concepts which, when rightly understood as metaphysical rules of the spiritual road, facilitate the individual's seeking. They need not be blindly believed, but it helps to accept them provisionally–that is, with an open mind and the understanding that in time the seeker will come to know for himself their truth and relevance.

The three eternals

Saint Thomas Christians believe that there are three eternal things: God, the individual spirits living within the greater Being of God, and the Creative Power that manifests as the relative existence within which the spirits evolve.

God

God is the ever-existent Spirit, the Absolute Consciousness that encompasses all things but is encompassed by none. Therefore God is totally beyond the reach of the human intellect and utterly indefinable or intellectually comprehensible. We can easily say what God is *not*–for anything we might say will not express him; but we cannot say a single word about what he *is*.

In Vedic religion, Sanatana Dharma, God is referred to as Brahman, the Absolute Being that is transcendent and beyond any qualities or conditionings whatsoever. However, with the inconsistency that is a marked trait of Eastern thinking, the ancient seers have given us a definition that enables us to get as much of a grasp of God as is possible for our minds. God is said to be *Sat-Chit-Ananda*: Existence, Consciousness, and Bliss.

Sat

God does not exist in the sense that things in relativity exist. Rather, he is existence itself. Or, more to the point, God is the very ground, the basis, of existence, in and through which all things exist. He is the ocean and all else are the waves. "He shining, all things shine," says the Veda, and: "His shadow is immortality." God can equally fittingly be called Reality itself.

Chit

God is Pure Consciousness, the very Principle of Consciousness itself. He is therefore omniscient–not in the sense of just knowing all things in the present moment, but in the sense of knowing all things whatsoever–past, present, and future–simultaneously. This is because God is outside of time and all things are present to him; nothing is past and nothing is future. God *is* the Eternal Now. Since all things are known to him, we can say that God is conscious, as well.

Ananda

"God is ever-new joy." This was the definition of God given by the great Master, Paramhansa Yogananda. God is not joyful, he is joy itself. God, then, is ever-existent, infinitely-conscious bliss.

Satchidananda

Satchidananda God is infinite, omnipresent, omniscient, and omnipotent; beginningless and endless; trinity and unity. Totally outside all things and yet within all things simultaneously. It is this latter statement that gives us a clue as to what we mean by the symbolic titles Father and Son. When we think of God as outside all things we say "Father," and when we think of God as within all things we say "the Son." But it is the one and only God we are speaking of in this way.

It can further be said that when the consciousness of God is turned inward upon his innate status as Satchidananda, we say "the Father;" and when the consciousness of God is turned outward toward creation and all things, we call that emanation or expansion of God "the Son." In some Indian texts we find the expression *Mahat Tattwa* which means that the Son is the emanation-reflection of the Father within creation, or in the mirror of creation–primordial matter (mulaprakriti).

For anything–including God–to exist in a relative manner there must be a duality, a polarization into positive and negative. Thus, at the very moment of emanation That which has emanated becomes divided into Two: Son and Holy Spirit, the Son being the Divine Positive and the Holy Spirit being the Divine Negative, though both are the Negative to the Positive of God the Father.

Primordial Energy (Mulaprakriti or Mahashakti), the Holy Spirit

God as consciousness is the eternal witness, but he is also the eternal actor or creator. And this he accomplishes through his kriya shakti (power of action) known as prakriti, the primordial power or energy, the Holy Breath, the Holy Spirit. This boundless field of vibrating energy is like an ocean which manifests in many waves. Whatever exists is made up of the endless variations of this primal energy. All that can be objectively experienced (and much that *seems* to be internally experienced, but is actually subtle objectivity) is formed of this divine energy. For Prakriti is not an unconscious or inert substance like a cosmic clay which God sculpts, but is God himself in the form of light, divine radiance.

We can think of it in this way: God by his very nature emits light, the Brahmajyoti; that this radiance ever streams forth from him eternally and boundlessly. And this light, "the true light, which lighteth every man that cometh into the world" (John 1:9), is itself conscious, for it is God. In the fourteenth century the great Greek theologian-mystic Saint Gregory Palamas wrote about how, without violating in any way his unity, God is both essence and energies in an incomprehensible way. Not that his energies are some kind of external or separate thing–rather it is an extension or expansion of God. Brahman, the Vedic word for God, comes from the root *brih*, which means "to expand," so this very idea is implied in Vedic religion as well.

Duality (and Trinity) in the Oneness of God

God is sometimes spoken of as "the Cosmic Egg" in the sense that he is the seed or germ of all life. Specifically, he is called Hiranyagarbha, the Golden Egg, for he shines, sending forth the radiance (tejas) that is the Great Energy, Mahashakti. And this energy is not an agent or instrument of God, but *is* God. Thus God is both absolutely one and absolutely two. This state of things is referred to in a mantra that is recited daily by Hindus:

Purnamidah, purnamidam,
purnat purnamudachyate;

Purnasya purnamadaya,
purnam ewawashishyate.

Purna means "total, full, complete," which is what our English term "perfect" used to mean, rather than just "without fault." In this verse, the word "complete" (purna) refers to God. Here, as best I can, is a translation into English:

This is the Complete; That is the Complete.
The Complete has come out of the Complete.
If we take the Complete away from the Complete,
Only the Complete remains.

Let us say it another way: the Absolute is the Totality; the Relative is the Totality. The Relative has emanated from the Absolute. Yet if we take away either of these and consider only the one or the other, we will find that each is the Totality; even more, we will discover that the Absolute is the Relative, and the Relative is the Absolute.

We can say it still another way: the Son is infinite God, the Father is infinite God. The Son has emanated from the Father. If we consider the Father alone, we will discover he is all there is of the Godhead, and is the Son as well. If we do the same with the Son, we will find that he is all there is of the Godhead, and is the Father. The same is true of the Holy Spirit, also.

It may tend to make our heads spin, but we have to realize that the unity and the duality (or trinity) are equally true, and that to ascribe either unity or duality (or trinity) to God exclusive of the other is to be mistaken. When we really know the Son, we know the Son is the Father, and when we really know the Father, we know the Father is the Son. When we really know the Holy Spirit we know she is the Father, the Son, and herself! To reject one is to reject the other(s), to accept one is to accept the other(s). For they are truly one.

Another point brought out by this is the impossibility of any actual conflict between the views of God as personal or impersonal, immanent or transcendent. The person who knows the impersonal knows that also is the personal. And those who know the personal know that he and she are also the impersonal.

Back to Satchidananda

Satchidananda also indicates the triune nature of God (Reality). Sat refers to God the Father, the transcendent absolute. Chit refers to God the Son, who is conscious of both the Father and the Holy Spirit as well as all "things" within them, including the individual souls such as you and me. Ananda refers to the Holy Spirit, the Mother, the vibrating power of God, the whole range of relative existence within whose womb are contained those souls that are evolving unto the status of sons of God. Both the coming into and the departing from her realm are births given the souls by their true Mother, the Holy Spirit.

Om Tat Sat

Om Tat Sat is a mantric formula usually spoken at the end of some act as a dedication of that act to God. It, too, refers to the Trinity, but in a different order. Om is the indicator of cosmic vibration itself and so refers to the vibratory divine life that is the Holy Spirit. Tat–which means "that"–refers to the Son whom we can speak of and even perceive as an object. Sat is "the real" (or "the true") that is existence itself, and consequently refers to the Father.

The individual souls (jivas)

You and I are part of the second eternal. We are gods, exact images of *the* God, also consisting of three aspects that are a miniature Trinity. We, too, consist of consciousness and energy, and our consciousness is also divided into father and son. That is, we are resting in the awareness of our own purely spiritual being and at the same time we are aware of our own tejas-radiance that is an extension of our own self as vibratory energy (shakti). Just as God is clothed in the evolving universe of many levels–physical, astral, and causal–so we are clothed in the various energy levels that are usually called "bodies."

As human beings we presently have five bodies (coverings or koshas): the annamaya, pranamaya, manomaya, jnanamaya, and anandamaya koshas. The annamaya body is the physical body formed of atomic matter. The pranamaya body consists of neurological and biomagnetic energies and is the seat of the emotions. The manomaya body is the energy field that is the sensory or percepting mind. The jnanamaya body is the even subtler energy field that is the intellect (sometimes called the buddhi). The anandamaya body is the primal energy that manifests as the will. All of these have many more aspects than outlined here, and they all consist of many layers within themselves, very much like an onion. All are composed of our personal energy field and are pervaded by our objective consciousness that is the Son as distinguished from our subjective consciousness that is the Father.

In the upanishads it is stated that the human being is like a fruit tree in which two birds are sitting. One bird is eating the fruit of the tree while the other witnesses–and actually experiences–its eating. The tree and its fruit are our bodies; the bird that eats the fruit is the aspect of our consciousness that is involved in external experience; and the other bird is the silent witness aspect of our consciousness untouched by all phenomena–perceiving all, but perceived by none but itself and God. This simile also can be applied to the archetypal Trinity.

It should be understood that God is conscious of creation, and we are conscious of our bodies and the creation with which they come into contact, because creation and our bodies are actually themselves consciousness: extensions of God and us. Although often appearing (acting) as inert and unconscious, the energy of which all things consist is intelligent consciousness. This is essential for our understanding of the who and the what of ourselves as well as our reactions to all things.

The souls and their energies exist eternally in God. Originally we were in the Bosom of the Father (John 1:18), within the very heart or depths of the infinite consciousness that is God. But, since we are image-reflections of that God whose very nature is action through the evolving creation, we, too, seek to evolve beyond our innate finite scope of consciousness in order to develop the capacity to experience infinite consciousness, the very consciousness of God. We cannot become God, but through the evolution of our various bodies we can develop the ability to share in the limitless being and consciousness that is the essential being of God. We can come to see with the eye of God, to hear with the ear of God, to think with the mind of God, and to know with the consciousness of God.

To accomplish this the individual soul comes out from the heart of God and enters into the creation, the dynamic life of the Holy Spirit. In this way it begins, through a series of rebirths, a seemingly infinite chain of manifestation-embodiments, evolving through increasingly complex forms to expand its innate capacity for experience, until it reaches the point where it can consciously re-enter the realm of God and participate fully in the divine omnipresence, omniscience, and omnipotence. The soul thus becomes totally godlike, but in no way does it become God. It becomes *one* with God, but it does not become the *same* as God. A soul that has attained this state is rightly called a son of God. And if such a one returns to earth to help others to attain the same status he is an avatara, a divine incarnation, who can say with the Lord Jesus: "To him that overcometh will I grant to sit with me in my throne, *even as I also overcame,* and am set down with my Father in his throne" (Revelation 3:21).

The soul and its destiny

The nature of the soul is as much an incomprehensible mystery to the intellect as is the nature of God. This is because both are eternal–and therefore beyond the grasp of the temporal intellect–and both are one.

The nature of that oneness is equally incomprehensible. Throughout the ages multitudes have pointlessly wrangled with one another over definitions of this oneness which by its very nature is indefinable.

It is the teaching of Saint Thomas Christianity that the existence of the individual spirit is rooted in God, the infinite Spirit, that God is himself the root of the individual spirit's existence. Yet a distinction exists. God encompasses all individual spirits, but none encompass him. God and the individual spirit are not two, but one. Yet there is a distinction between them. The great Master Tung-Shan, founder of the Soto school of Zen Buddhism, wrote:

> If you look for the truth outside yourself,
> it gets farther and farther away.
> Today, walking alone, I meet him everywhere I step.
> He is the same as me, yet I am not him.
> Only if you understand it in this way
> will you merge with the way things are.

(Note how theistic this poem is despite the modern insistence that Zen is atheistic.)

As has been said, this status is simply incomprehensible. There is eternal unity and there is eternal diversity. Yet this diversity is not in any sense a duality. The individual spirits are absolutely and irrevocably inseparable from God. There is the beginningless and endless existence of God and all spirits. There is also the distinction-within-unity that is the present and eternal status of the individualized spirits in relation to God. There was never a time when the individualized spirits did not exist as individualized spirits, nor at any time in the future shall this mode of existence cease to be, as Krishna states in the Bhagavad Gita (2:12). What shall cease to be is the limitation of consciousness when the individual spirits attain perfect unity with God in the sharing of his omniscience, omnipresence, and omnipotence.

"Be ye therefore perfect, even as your Father which is in heaven is perfect" (Matthew 5:48). The true Gospel of Christ is the call to divine perfection, to the "knowledge of the Son of God, unto a perfect man, unto the measure of the stature of the fulness of Christ" (Ephesians 4:13). It is this "Christ in you, the hope of glory" (Colossians 1:27), which impels the Saint Thomas Christian to affirm: "But we all, with open face beholding as in a glass [mirror] the glory of the Lord, are changed into the same image from glory to glory, even as by the Spirit of the Lord" (II Corinthians 3:18). "Beloved, now are we the sons of God, and it doth not yet appear what we shall be: but we know that, when he shall appear, we shall be like him; for we shall see him as he is" (I John 3:2).

Simple as it is, Swami Dayananda Saraswati's statement regarding the status of the sons of God is perhaps the best: "They consciously live and move freely and without limit within God." This is supported by the following experience of Saint Ambrose of Optina, a Russian Orthodox saint of the last century.

The vision of Saint Ambrose

"Suddenly I was in another world, quite unknown to me, never seen by me, never imagined by me. Around me there is bright, white light! Its transcendence is so pure and enticing that I am submerged, along with my perception, into limitless depths and cannot satisfy myself with my admiration for this realm, cannot completely fill myself with its lofty spirituality. Everything is so full of beauty all around. So endearing this life—so endless the way. I am being swept across this limitless, clear space. My sight is directed upwards, does not descend anymore, does not see anything earthly. The whole of the heavenly firmament has transformed itself before me into one general bright light, pleasing to the sight.

"But I do not see the sun. I can see only its endless shining and bright light. The whole space in which I glide without hindrance, without end, without fatigue, is filled with white light, just as is its light and beautiful beings, transparent as a ray of the sun. And through them I am admiring this limitless world. The images of all these beings unknown to me are infinitely diverse and full of beauty.

"I also am white and bright as they are. Over me, as over them, there reigns eternal rest. Not a single thought of mine is any longer enticed by anything earthly, not a single beat of my heart is any longer moving with human cares or earthly passion. I am all peace and rapture. But I am still moving in this infinite light, which surrounds me without change. There is nothing else in the world except for the white, bright light and these equally radiant numberless beings. But all these beings do not resemble me, nor are similar to each other; they are all endlessly varied and compellingly attractive. Amidst them, I feel myself incredibly peaceful. They evoke in me neither fear, nor amazement, nor trepidation. All that we see here does not agitate us, does not amaze us. All of us here are as if we have belonged to each other for a long time, are used to each other and are not strangers at all. We do not ask questions, we do not speak to each other about anything. We all feel and understand that there is nothing novel for us here. All our questions are solved with one glance, which sees everything and everyone. There is no trace of the wars of passions in anyone. All move in different directions, opposite to each other, not feeling any limitation, any inequality, or envy, or sorrow, or sadness. One peace reigns in all the images of entities. One light is endless for all. Oneness of life is comprehensible to all.

"My rapture at all this superseded everything. I sank into this eternal rest. No longer was my spirit disturbed by anything. And I knew nothing else earthly. None of the tribulations of my heart came to mind, even for a minute. It seemed that everything that I had experienced before on earth never existed. Such was my feeling in this new radiant world of mine. And I was at peace and joyful and desired nothing better for myself. All my earthly thoughts concerning fleeting happiness in the world died in this beautiful life, new to me, and did not come back to life again. So it seemed to me at least, there, in that better world.

"But how I came back here—I do not recall. What transitory state it was, I do not know. I only felt that I was alive, but I did not remember the world in which I lived before on earth. This did not seem at all to be a dream. Actually, about earthly things I no longer had the least notion. I only felt that the present life is *mine*, and that *I* was not a stranger in it. In this state of spirit I forgot myself and immersed myself in this light-bearing eternity. And this timelessness lasted without end, without measure, without expectation, without sleep, in this eternal rest. Thus it seemed to me that there would not be any kind of change." For this is what is meant in the book of Job about that state "when the morning stars sing together, and all the sons of God shout for joy" (Job 38:7).

The Three are One

Before leaving this subject of the three eternals we should recall that from the standpoint of God these three are one in an incomprehensible manner, though from the standpoint of the individual soul these three are distinct from one another. The Ocean of God is one, but the waves of creation and the souls are many. The great non-dual philosopher Shankaracharya wrote: "O Lord, although we are one, I belong to You, but You do not belong to me. For the ocean can say 'I am the wave,' but the wave cannot say 'I am the ocean.'" The Master Yogananda used to say that we can say "God has become me," but we cannot say "I am God." Accordingly, Saint Thomas Christians consider that the viewpoints of Advaita (Non-dualism), Vashistadvaita (Qualified Non-dualism), and Dwaita (Dualism) are all three true when taken together, but that when one or two of them is ignored or overemphasized error is the result. Furthermore, no one of the three is *the* right, best, or highest view. For ultimately all viewing vanishes into *being*.

This entire process of evolution that has been set forth above is possible only through the two laws of reincarnation and karma.

Reincarnation

Although reincarnation is commonly represented in the West as being an exclusively Hindu or Buddhist belief, it is not. (See *May a Christian Believe in Reincarnation?*) Reincarnation is a tenet of orthodox Judaism, wherein it is called *gilgul* or *ha'atakah*, and was so at the time of Jesus.

"And as Jesus passed by, he saw a man which was blind from his birth. And his disciples asked him, saying, Master, who did sin, this man, or his parents, that he was born blind? Jesus answered, Neither hath this man sinned, nor his parents: but that the works of God should be made manifest in him" (John 9:1-3).

In this passage we learn that the Apostles of Jesus believed that a person's situation in life is determined by his actions–in this case seemingly negative–committed before birth: that is, in a previous life. Although the man's blindness was for the glory of God, the Lord said, "neither hath this man sinned, nor his parents," implying that the man had certainly existed, and been capable of sinning, before the present birth in which he was blind.

Speaking to a crowd about John the Baptist, Jesus told them: "This is he, of whom it is written, Behold, I send my messenger before thy face, which shall prepare thy way before thee.…And if you will receive it, this is Elias which was for to come" (Matthew 11:10, 14). Later "His disciples asked him, saying, Why then say the scribes that Elias must first come? And Jesus answered and said unto them,…I say to you, That Elias is come already, and they knew him not, but have done unto him whatsoever they listed.…Then the disciples understood that he spake unto them of John the Baptist" (Matthew 17:10, 12, 13).

The purpose of reincarnation is for us to grow and evolve spiritually until we return to the Godhead from whence we came. Each life is the result of the ones preceding it and is shaped accordingly–not in the sense of reward or punishment, but as precise mathematical reaction to our actions in those previous lives. We reap what we sowed in them through the exercise of our free wills. Though we may forget it, we are at all times masters of our destiny and not at all swept along blindly by karma–which is really our own creation.

Equally, if not more important, is the fact that every experience and action in our previous births produces a shaping of our personal energies which manifest mostly as the personality. These shapings, called *samskaras*, are likened to impressions made in wax or clay that momentarily impart a distinctive shape or character, yet are erased and overwritten with other impressions in an endless succession of changes. So karma and samskara are the two determinants of the quality and character of each reincarnation.

The implication of karma

The individual soul, being endowed with free, creative will according to the divine image, must also shoulder the responsibility for that will–the responsibility being in the form of the irrevocable law: "Whatsoever a man soweth, that shall he also reap" (Galatians 6:7). The law is that we must receive back *whatever* we sow, not just some kind of reaction. This is reinforced by God's own words when he told Noah: "Whoso sheddeth man's blood, by man shall his blood be shed" (Genesis 9:6). Retribution must be in the form of experiencing exactly what we have done to others–no substitute. For the Lord Jesus was not just putting forth a social directive when he said: "Whatsoever ye would that men should do to you, do ye even so to them" (Matthew 7:12). He was simply restating the Law that whatever you do to others will in turn be done to you. And since "he that soweth to his flesh shall *of the flesh* reap" (Galatians 6:8), reincarnation is an absolute necessity, to provide us the flesh in which to reap what we have sown. It would be appropriate for a Saint Thomas Christian to use the term "sowing and reaping," but "karma" is much shorter.

As said earlier, Saint Thomas Christians hold that the twin laws of karma and rebirth as understood in Hinduism are the fundamental truths about human existence, and without them no religious or personal philosophy can be either true or viable.

Who was—and is—Jesus?

In Vedic religion it is believed that the human race had more than one set of foreparents. It appears from the accounts given in Genesis that the inhabitants of the Mesopatamian and Mediterranean areas as well as those regions to their north were the descendants of Adam and Eve. These are the very people that, without exception, became Christians in the first centuries after Christ. The reason is evident: their profound ancestral link to Jesus. (See *Robe of Light*.)

The *Nishmath Chaim* (Fol. 152, col. 2), a book contemporary with Jesus and the Apostles which would have been studied by Saint Paul, says: "The sages of truth remark that Adam contains the initial letters of Adam, David, and Messiah; for after Adam sinned his soul passed into David, and the latter having also sinned, it passed into the Messiah."

He who was Jesus of Nazareth was Adam. When Adam "fell," he was in Paradise, the astral plane immediately above the physical creation. But the alteration in consciousness which resulted from his transgression rendered him unable to function in that subtle world, so he sank back down into the physical plane, through which he had already evolved before entering Paradise. In Genesis we read: "And for Adam and his wife the Lord God made tunics of skin, and clothed them" (Genesis 4:21). Although many now take this to mean that they were given clothes like the cavemen are depicted wearing, Christians originally understood that the real meaning of this verse was that God created physical bodies—the human organism—for Adam and Eve to inhabit, and thus they continued in the cycle of life, death, and rebirth upon the earth.

The Old Testament is the account of Adam's evolving to become the Christ. Adam evolved through life after life as Noah, Abraham, Joseph, Moses, David, Elisha, and Isaiah. Ascending to and evolving beyond higher and higher worlds, at last he passed through the final barrier of the angelic (seraphic) planes and attained perfect union with the Father/Son aspect of God. From this point the soul normally passes into total union with the pure, transcendent Being of the Father, ending the evolutionary cycle, but it was not so for Adam. He was in debt: a debt owed to all of his descendants, one of such magnitude that it could only be paid by one of infinite consciousness–which Adam now was.

So Adam returned, of necessity, to our earth plane in his earthly incarnation as Jesus of Nazareth, the Christ (Messiah)–not only paying the debt, but showing and opening the way to the Father for his children, many of whom were, through rebirth, by that time scattered throughout the earth.

When Jesus told his apostles to make disciples among all nations he was not meaning that the whole world was to be converted to Christianity, but that they should seek out those who in past lives had been his descendants and been negatively affected by the fall of Adam. He was referring to them when he had told them: "Other sheep I have, which are not of this fold [of Israel]: them also I must bring, and they shall hear my voice; and there shall be one fold, and one shepherd" (John 10:16). He did not mean that the entire human race was to become Christian.

When Saint Paul speaks of Jesus as being the "second man [Adam]… from heaven" (I Corinthians 15:47). he speaks quite literally, and not figuratively. He also speaks literally about Adam paying his debt: "For since by man came death, by man came also the resurrection of the dead. For as in Adam all die, even so in Christ shall all be made alive" (I Corinthians 15:21, 22). Does this mean, then, that Jesus is only a man, and not the Son of God? No. Jesus positively *is* the Son of God. And so shall we all be Sons of God like him. But first he was a man–one of the foreparents of the human race, as we have said. Then he ascended to divinity, attaining perfect union with God.

The real good news (which is what "gospel" means) is that as Adam passed from fallen ignorance and sin unto perfect Divinity, so shall his disciples do the same through him. Jesus affirmed this when he told the Apostles: "Be of good cheer; *I have overcome the world*" (John 16:33). Later, to his Beloved Apostle John, he said: "To him that overcometh will I grant to sit with me in my throne, *even as I also overcame,* and am set down with my Father in his throne" (Revelation 3:21). As it was with Jesus, so shall it be with us. The passage from humanity to divinity–to Christhood–is the real essence of Saint Thomas Christian belief. The life of the Lord Jesus as given in the four Gospels is also a symbolic mystery-drama showing how the soul of each person becomes a Christ–an anointed of the Lord.

Again, we are saying that Jesus the Christ was *once* a human being just like us, but is now in the status of Son of God, just as we shall be. Saint John wrote: "Beloved, now are we the sons of God, and it doth not yet appear what we shall be: but we know that, when he shall appear, we shall be like him; for we shall see him as he is" (I John 3:2). That is, when we "see" God (the Father) through union with him, we shall be perfectly transmuted into his image and likeness and thus truly become the sons of God, hearing the words: "Thou art my Son; this day have I begotten thee" (Psalms 2:7, Acts 13:33, Hebrews 1:5, 5:5) in mystic vision. This is the very thing that happened to Adam/Jesus, which is why he is called "the first-fruits of them that slept" (I Corinthians 15:20).

What is Jesus to the Saint Thomas Christians?

Saint Thomas Christians worship only God, to Whom Jesus has pointed them. Therefore they love and revere him without reservation in the way that other sampradayas, such as those of Shankara, Ramanuja, and Madhavacharya, honor and even venerate their founder-acharyas. But they remember Saint Paul's plain statement that Jesus is "the firstborn among many brethren" (Romans 8:29). That is, he is our Elder Brother. "For both he that sanctifieth and they who are sanctified are all of one: for which cause he is not ashamed to call them brethren" (Hebrews 2:11). Because we and Jesus are "all of one"–that is, of one nature as individual souls, we are his brethren. In India the eldest brother is given respect almost equal to the father of the household. Saint Thomas Christians therefore give supreme honor to Lord Jesus, but they do not mistake the son for the Father.

He himself has also told us that we are his friends (John 15:13, 14), and that "henceforth I call you not servants; for the servant knoweth not what his lord doeth: but I have called you friends; for all things that I have heard of my Father I have made known unto you" (John 15:15). For it is his intention that we should become exactly what he is. That this is possible, the Beloved Apostle makes clear when he says: "He that saith he abideth in him *ought himself also so to walk, even as he walked. And every man that hath this hope in him purifieth himself, even as he is pure*....He that doeth righteousness is righteous, *even as he is righteous*" (I John 2:6, 3:3, 7).

The Lord Jesus is to the Saint Thomas Christians a brother, friend, teacher and guide. He teaches them not only through his recorded words, but through the omniscience, omnipotence, and omnipresence of God in which he now shares. This being true, Jesus is the Master of each Saint Thomas Christian. For Jesus is ever present with and within them as an ever-living Presence. Each Saint Thomas Christian is as fully a disciple of Jesus as was Saint Thomas. Hence Jesus is verily the Way, the Truth, and the Life of each Saint Thomas Christian in his journey back to the Father (John 14:6).

The goal and the way

Saint Thomas Christianity holds out only one goal to its initiates: the realization and manifestation of their innate Christhood. Jesus the Christ of Nazareth came to earth to reveal the Christhood which is the destiny of every person. It is our own personal Christhood that is our Savior, as Saint Paul said: "Christ *in you,* the hope of glory." But this inner Christ must be awakened and developed unto perfection. This is accomplished by the means of empowerment and spiritual enlightenment known as the sacraments, and especially by the practice of meditation.

In the opening of his Gospel, Saint John wrote: "As many as received him, to them gave he power to become the sons of God" (John 1:12). "In all things it behoved him to be made like unto his brethren" (Hebrews

2:17). Jesus became like us in all things, and through the sacraments and meditation we are empowered to "grow up into him in all things," (Ephesians 4:15), becoming like Saint Thomas his "twin" in all things. For that is what it means to be a "Saint Thomas Christian." We become interpenetrated with the Christ Consciousness of Jesus and assimilate It into our own consciousness.

This accomplishes the following five things within the individual disciple:

1. It frees him from negative psychic bonds.
2. It deeply cleanses him from the negative energy patterns ("sins") which have been stored up in his physical and psychic bodies from his past lives as well as the present one and that have hitherto obscured his spiritual vision.
3. All of his bodies are infused with positive energies, attuning and enlivening them for his conscious spiritual growth.
4. Every atom of his physical and psychic makeup is clothed in the divine creative Light that is the Holy Spirit, empowering them for the fullest degree of evolution.
5. An entirely new dimension is added to his being in which he can begin to function in the higher worlds while yet on the earth plane.

Such a process is both a rebirth and a re-creation. "Another parable spake he unto them; The kingdom of heaven is like unto leaven, which a woman took, and hid in three measures of meal, till the whole was leavened" (Matthew 13:33). Consciousness begins to pervade all the levels of our being to awaken our own consciousness and transmute us into Christs, which is exactly what being a Christian is all about. What is needed is for us to "taste and see that the Lord is good" (Matthew 13:33).

Worship

The Holy Eucharist is their usual form of external worship, but true worship is understood by the Saint Thomas Christians as a means of linking lower consciousness with higher consciousness, the human with the divine. In Greek it is *proskuneo*, and in Sanskrit, *upasana*. *Upasana* means "to draw near." *Proskuneo* also means to draw near, but includes the idea of doing so with love. It is related to *prosekho*, which means to fix the awareness upon an object, to become conscious of something. From these three terms we gain an exact and pragmatic understanding of worship: the process of lovingly fixing our attention upon God and thereby being drawn closer into communication with him—not mere conversation or verbal exchange, but the communication to us of divine qualities and divine consciousness. In other words, true worship is an act which accomplishes an *assimilation* of higher consciousness. To rightly worship God is to become god—to bring about the union of our finite being with the infinite being in so perfect a unity that we can truthfully say with Jesus: "I and my Father are one" (John 10:30). Consequently, the Saint Thomas Christians consider that meditation is the most appropriate and effective worship of God.

In the tradition of the Christian East the word commonly used for meditation is the Greek word *Hesychia*: the Silence. Though usually translated "the silence," Hesychia also means "the stillness." A perfect symbol of this is given in the book of Acts: "He commanded the chariot to stand still: and they went down both into the water, both Philip and the eunuch; and he baptized him" (Acts 8:38). To make the chariot of the mind stand still and descend into the stream of the inmost consciousness, to be baptized in the Silence, is to be baptized in Christ, in the Word, and to be truly Christed (Christened). "For as many of you as have been baptized into Christ have put on Christ" (Galatians 3:27).

Purification

The aspiration to Christhood is truly marvelous. And as Saint John the Beloved Disciple tells us, "every man that hath this hope in him purifieth himself, even as he is pure" (I John 3:3), for only the cleansed and purified mirror reflects the Divine Visage. Therefore purification—*continual* purification—is necessary for those who aspire to regain their original purity of spirit, praying with Jesus: "O Father, glorify with thine own self with the glory which I had with thee b world was" (John 17:5).

Purification takes many forms, but for the Saint Thomas Christian it is purification and refinement of the energies of his various levels of being–physical, astral, and causal–that is of major importance in his endeavor for spiritual transmutation. This being so, purification of the body is essential, especially through observance of personal morality–a life led according to the principles of moral purity.

Truth and morality

Truth is the basis of the Saint Thomas Christian's moral purity– truthfulness with himself and with others. For this reason he does his best to always speak and think the truth, as well as to live out the principles of truth in all aspects of his life. Honesty in all his dealings with others–especially in the making of his livelihood–is an extension of his commitment to truth. Application of the Ten Commandments and the Beatitudes–understood in both their exoteric and esoteric meanings– form the basis of his life in the material and spiritual realms. (*The Gnosis of the Ten Commandments and the Beatitudes* on our website contains full expositions of the esoteric nature of the Ten Commandments and the Beatitudes.)

Of prime importance are Ten Commandments of Yoga, the Five Abstentions (Yama) and the Five Observances (Niyama) mandated in Patanjali's Yoga Sutras. They are:

1. ahimsa–non-violence, non-injury, harmlessness
2. satya–truthfulness, honesty
3. asteya–non-stealing, honesty, non-misappropriativeness
4. brahmacharya–continence
5. aparigraha–non-possessiveness, non-greed, non-selfishness, non-acquisitiveness
6. shaucha–purity, cleanliness

7. santosha–contentment, peacefulness
8. tapas–austerity, practical (i.e., result-producing) spiritual discipline
9. swadhyaya–introspective self-study, spiritual study
10. Ishwarapranidhana–offering of one's life to God

Dietary purity

"Hearken diligently unto me, and eat ye that which is good, and let your soul delight itself" (Isaiah 55:2). All levels of our personal being, from the physical body to the subtle energy levels known as the astral and causal bodies, are derived almost exclusively from food. Our spiritual quest is therefore greatly facilitated by wise eating–that is, by the diet that best supports the quest for conscious evolution and the attainment of the highest states of consciousness. That quest and attainment demand a degree of purification that can only be achieved through total abstinence from meat (including fish and eggs), alcohol, nicotine, and mind-altering drugs (legal or otherwise). Because of their darkening, deadening, and paralyzing psychic effects, these substances are known as the Four Soul Killers.

Abstinence from the Four Soul Killers is essential for the fundamental purification, stabilization, and strengthening of the outer and inner bodies–whose very substance is drawn from food. An aspirant to Christhood must break his addiction to those destructive things. And perpetual abstinence is necessary to maintain the transformative spiritual life. Since we are dealing with evolution which occurs neither by whim nor mere wish, but by precise laws, the need for such abstinence cannot be mitigated or abrogated.

A full presentation of the esoteric rationale behind the need for purity of diet is found in *Christian Vegetarianism* and *The Four Soul Killers* on our website, but here are some basic points:

1. God not only created humans and animals, he decreed the diet for them. "And God said, Behold, I have given you every herb bearing seed, which is upon the face of all the earth, and every tree, in the which is

the fruit of a tree yielding seed; *to you it shall be for meat.* And to every beast of the earth, and to every fowl of the air, and to every thing that creepeth upon the earth, wherein there is life, *I have given every green herb for meat:* and it was so" (Genesis 1:29, 30). From this we see that neither humans nor animals are natural flesh-eaters. To be so is to violate the divine pattern.

2. The eating of meat directly opposes the commandment: "Thou shalt not kill" (Exodus 20:13). God did not qualify his prohibition by adding the words: "human beings." Killing is prohibited strictly "across the board." The Hebrew word translated "kill" is *tirtzach*, which according to *The Complete Hebrew/English Dictionary* means: "any kind of killing whatsoever."

3. God himself has spoken on the severity of slaughtering cattle: "He that killeth an ox is as if he slew a man" (Isaiah 66:3). No need for interpretation. It is quite clear: to kill a cow is as homicide in God's eyes. Why? Because that cow is as real and viable a person as you and I, with just as much right to earth life for evolution as anyone else. And if we do not think that God values cattle with humans, consider his words to Jonah: "Should I not pity Ninevah, that great city, wherein are more than six score thousand persons that cannot discern between their right hand and their left hand; *and also much cattle?*" (Jonah 4:11).

4. "For meat destroy not the work of God. All things indeed are pure; but it is evil for that man who eateth with offense. It is good neither to eat meat or drink wine...." (Romans 14:20, 21).

5. The oldest known version of the Gospels is in Aramaic, the actual language which Christ spoke. The text of Luke 21:34 in this version reads: "Now take care in your souls that you *never* make your hearts heavy *by eating flesh and by drinking wine.*"

In the early centuries of Christianity vegetarianism was the norm according to such authoritative persons as Saint Jerome, Papias, Tertullian, Saint Benedict, Saint Clement, Eusebius, Saint John Chrysostom, Saint Cyprian, Saint Pantaenus, and Saint Basil the Great. Their words on the subject are found in *Christian Vegetarianism* and *The Four Soul Killers*. In a homily on the Gospel of Matthew, Saint John Chrysostom said: "Flesh meats and wine serve as materials for sensuality and are a source of danger, sorrow, and disease." Saint Jerome, virtually quoting Saint Paul, wrote: "It is a good thing not to drink wine and not to eat flesh." Saint Basil the Great wrote: "With sober living, well-being increases in the household, animals are in safety, there is no shedding of blood, nor putting animals to death." The historian Hegesippus records that Saint James of Jerusalem "drank no wine nor strong drink, nor did he eat flesh." Origen wrote: "I believe that animal sacrifices were invented by men to be a pretext for eating flesh."

The great miracle-worker, Saint John of Kronstadt, in his diaries wrote forcefully and uncompromisingly about the incompatibility of meat-eating with spiritual life. For example: "It is better to avoid meat, which turns you into an animal." He would accept no one as a spiritual student unless they took a vow to never eat meat, for he said that the more someone lives in God the less they will eat meat. And since the goal is to live completely in God, the wise stop eating meat altogether right at the beginning of spiritual life.

In point of fact, all the Saint Thomas Christian spiritual practices–particularly meditation–require a clarity and subtlety of perception that can only be obtained through scrupulous abstinence from meat, fish, eggs, nicotine, alcohol, and mind-affecting drugs. The pure and life-supporting elements of vegetables, grains, fruits, pure water, and juices constitute the diet of the Saint Thomas Christian. In this way he fosters his physical, mental, and spiritual health.

One of the most important effects of a pure diet is the ease and effectiveness the Saint Thomas Christian experiences in his practice of meditation and the other spiritual observances. For this reason–and not from prejudice or mere disciplinary stringency–strict dietary abstinence is one of the most valuable aspects of the Saint Thomas Christian's life. Fortunately, the positive effects of a pure diet are soon perceived by him.

The most important part of the Saint Thomas Christian's diet is his spiritual diet: the practice of meditation through which he expands his consciousness, receives ineffable enlivening within all the levels of his being, and enters into communion with God–thus working steadily toward the revelation of his own Christhood.

(For the health aspect of vegetarianism, I recommend *What's Wrong With Eating Meat?* by Vistara Parham (PCAP Publications, Corona, New York), and *Diet For a New America* by John Robbins (Stillpoint Publishing, Walpole, New Hampshire.)

Life in the Spirit

All these observances are beneficial to the Saint Thomas Christian in ways unrealized until they are put into practice. Then they are the wings on which he rises to his goal, opening for himself the pathways to higher consciousness. If the right seeds are sown now, in time we shall reap the harvest of everlasting life.

"If we live in the Spirit, let us also walk in the Spirit" (Galatians 5:25).

The keys of the kingdom

Matter is derived from spirit–is a manifestation of spirit. Therefore when Jesus told his disciples: "I will give unto thee the keys of the kingdom of heaven" (Matthew 16:19), he was speaking of those esoteric rituals known as Sacraments involving material elements that produce transformation of the physical, psychic and spiritual levels of those initiated into and by them. For an in-depth analysis of those rites, please read *The Yoga of the Sacraments*, for here just a simple outline must suffice.

Baptism is a ritual of profound purification based on oil and water that have been infused with spiritual powers. Since the human body itself is mostly oil and water, when the oil is applied to it and it is washed with the water, tremendous power flows out of those elements into the body, mind and spirit of the initiate.

Confirmation (Chrismation) is the empowerment of the initiate who has been prepared for it by Baptism. At the touch of the bishop's hand and the holy Chrism, the Holy Spirit pours into the crown chakra (brahmarandhra) of the initiate and fills his entire being on all levels, making him a literal temple of the Holy Spirit. Through this Sacrament the light body which Adam and Eve lost in their transgression is restored to him and he becomes a dweller both in the earth and in Paradise. Those who have been baptized and confirmed and have subsequently fostered that grace are normal human beings, restored to their original divine image and likeness. They are potential gods.

The Holy Eucharist (Mass) builds on the foundation of Baptism and Chrismation to further the spiritualization of the initiate. The elements of those two Sacraments were filled with divine power. In the Eucharist the offered elements of bread and (unfermented) wine become vehicles for the divine Consciousness of Christ which manifested as his resurrected Presence. The communicants then receive these elements and unite themselves with the Christ in both Jesus and themselves.

The other Sacraments such as Anointing of the Sick are adjuncts to these three life-giving rituals and support and maintain their effects.

Without cultivation of interior consciousness through meditation and the disciplines that foster inner awakening, the Sacraments can do very little good, if any. Two thousand years of exoteric Christianity have demonstrated that. Yet they are necessary for those who would follow the Way of Christ by cultivating an interior and exterior Christ Life.

The Saint Thomas Christian View of Dharma

"All the religions of the world have come into existence through the will of God, and all will cease to exist through His will. But the religion of India will never cease to exist, for it alone is the Sanatana [Eternal] Dharma." Sri Ramakrishna Paramhansa

The nature of dharma

First it must be stated that mere philosophy or theology is totally useless if it is not supported by a way of life that enables the individual to unfold and bring to perfection the qualities that are the eternal nature of every individual spirit or jiva. Those principles and practices which comprise such an enabling life are what we mean by dharma. A philosophical view is only a darshan, an intellectual view of the way things are. Such is necessary, but only as it leads to the mode of living that is dharma.

True dharma was directly perceived by the rishis of India. Known as Sanatana (Eternal) Dharma, it reveals the Eternal Being, the Sanatana Purusha. That which is in accord with Sanatana Dharma is true; that which is not is untrue, because Sanatana Dharma is not a religion: it is Truth. Religions are usually degenerations of truth and confuse the issue.

In India Sanatana Dharma and Hinduism are naturally considered synonymous, though certain sects are not fully in accord with Sanatana Dharma. For example: those who believe in everlasting damnation, such as the Madhavacharya Sampradaya; those who decry and denounce as either false or inferior all forms of deity other than their particular chosen form, such as certain sectarian Shaivites, Shaktas, and Vaishnavas; those that decry and denounce all forms of deity, such as the Radhaswami or Sant Mat sects. All of these usually denounce and decry all acharyas not of their sampradaya. Frankly, many of today's Hindu Fundamentalists are much more akin to Moslem and Christian fanatics than to real Hindus.

The following is our attempt to outline and define the philosophy of Sanatana Dharma as we understand and apply it as Saint Thomas Christians, though mere words can never fully express or encompass it adequately.

God (Brahman)

God, or Brahman, is Absolute Being, outside of which there can be nothing. As a consequence, all relative existence is essentially absolute existence, and as such is the divine reality in manifestation without any loss or alternation of its nature. Thus there is no such thing as creation from nothing.

The same is true of all the individual consciousnesses: spirit-selves or atmas. No one is, or can be, either mortal or sinful by nature. Rather, just as all the waves are formed of the ocean and are an inherent, inseparable part of the ocean, so all individuals or jivas are eternal parts of Brahman, the whole. Although Brahman is the totality of our being and existence, no one jiva can claim to be the totality of Brahman..

Nevertheless, each jiva is totally divine. Any experience or condition that contradicts or veils this is illusory (maya), and can be eradicated from the consciousness by the practice of yoga as revealed to and formulated by the ancient sages (rishis) of India such as Maharishi

Patanjali and Yogi Guru Gorakhnath. Realization of one's innate divinity is inevitable for each person (jiva). Jiva the individual is Shiva the Absolute.

World-view

Dharma includes a God-and-spirit-centric view of the world which affirms that all experiences of enlightenment and divine contact are open to every single human being; that no historical event of spiritual illumination and revelation is unique and unrepeatable *if it is authentic*. Further, that every spiritual aspirant who follows the path of yoga can verify for himself the truth or error of any statement of belief or unbelief, that blind acceptance of any tenet or individual as a source of spiritual knowledge is spiritually destructive, including demands of exclusivity for any religion or teacher.

Identity with Brahman (God)

Each individual consciousness or jiva not only exists within Brahman, Brahman is the inmost reality of each jiva. Seated within the heart of all, Brahman directs and brings about the awakening of each one. Although in our present state most persons require some kind of instruction and guidance from those who are more experienced in the path of yoga and dharma, it is God alone that enables and enlightens the jiva.

There is no one that can stand in the place of God and claim to represent God in our lives. As Buddha said, a true and worthy teacher (acharya) is only a finger pointing to the moon. God, and none other, is the moon, and the wise do not keep looking at the finger but focus attention on the moon.

Further, there is no philosophical or dogmatic formulation, no intellectual teaching or teacher, that is absolutely necessary for liberation (moksha), the only true salvation. Yoga, however, is necessary because it alone reveals and establishes us in our eternal nature. Moksha is our eternal nature and God is our eternal guru.

Three fundamental facts

There are three fundamental facts of our present existence:
1. The law of cause and effect, or action and reaction, expounded to us by the rishis as *karma*.
2. Karma renders necessary the experience of *rebirth or reincarnation* (punarjanma) in order for the individual to "reap" the effects of his karmic "sowing" in past, present, and future births. This, too, is a Law.
3. The purpose or effect of Karma and Rebirth is *evolution of consciousness*, the unfoldment of the jiva's inherent divinity. At first this takes place automatically, a virtual function of the cosmos (samsara), but in time the human status is reached after passing through countless lower forms of manifestation. After some time the human being becomes capable of taking charge of and accelerating his evolution through the methodology of classical yoga.

To accommodate these three preceding points, the cosmos perpetually passes through stages of manifestation and non-manifestation, the Days and Nights of Brahma. Furthermore, the cosmos is not just physical, but embraces many levels or layers of evolution and consciousness, through which every single jiva passes in its journey to the revelation of its pure nature as eternal Brahman.

Dharma is eternal

The principles of dharma, like the principles of mathematics, are both eternal and universal in their application.

Just as mathematics has no originator or author or connotation of any culture, the same is true of dharma. Dharma is discovered, not created by human beings. For example, "Euclidian Geometry" was discovered by the Greek Euclid, but it is not Greek in any way and carries no connotation of Hellenism.

Nevertheless, it cannot be responsibly denied that Sanatana Dharma, Eternal Truth or Religion, has been completely and perfectly imparted to us by the enlightened sages or rishis (seers) of India, many of whom are completely unknown to us by name. Their vision has been conveyed to us in various sacred texts, using Sanskrit as the perfect, exact and necessary vehicle for its expression. No one should presume the ability or the authority to declare which texts are or are not of supreme or exclusive authority, but we can feel secure in considering that the Upanishads, Bhagavad Gita, and the sutras on which the six orthodox Darshanas (Nyaya, Vaisheshika, Purva Mimamsa, Uttara Mimamsa or Vedanta, Sankhya, and Yoga) are based can be accepted as trustworthy guides. In addition there are numberless texts that transmit Sanatana Dharma to the seeker. These include the writings of great philosophers and yogis, ancient and modern. But the ones listed are of unquestioned reliability.

Dharma is universal

Wherever in the world we find any truth, philosophical or spiritual, it is a reflection of Sanatana Dharma, and is often evidence of a forgotten historical presence of India's influence in that part of the world. At the root of every valid religion we will find Sanatana Dharma–not just abstractly but as the historical presence just mentioned. For example, both Buddha and Jesus were nourished in the bosom of Sanatana Dharma–one as a "native son" and the other as a pilgrim seeker. Those who consider themselves their followers may have strayed far from the principles which produced and empowered those two great teachers, but that in no way dims their value as adherents of the Eternal Dharma. Those who would follow them must of necessity look to the same fountainhead of wisdom from which they drank and came to live–and honestly and openly acknowledge it.

India

No one is a follower of truth who does not accede to the teachings of the sages of India and their successors through untold centuries the position of primacy and even supremacy both philosophically and religiously. And this should be a personal evaluation, not a vague historical "appreciation." Further, it must be continually overt and obvious in their words and deeds, giving credit where credit is due. Recasting the teachings of Sanatana Dharma in forms seeming to be native to any other philosophy or religion is merely plagiarism, shameful and childish and often vicious.

Jesus a Siddha

Jesus Christ was not an orthodox Jew, but an Essene who had studied the wisdom of India in the Essene schools. (For this openness the Essenes were officially condemned by orthodox Judaism.) He spent most of his life in India and returned to Israel as a missionary of Sanatana Dharma. This book could not really be a presentation of original Christianity if it did not present the teachings of the Dharma which Jesus brought back from India.

Jesus Christ was God in the sense that as atmas we are all divine, but he was not the Creator God, nor was he a blood sacrifice to satisfy an angry God and draw his wrath away from humanity. Rather, he was a great Siddha, a liberated being who for all practical purposes can be called an avatara, an incarnation of God, as have been many others throughout history–especially in India.

Jesus' original contribution

There is one aspect of Jesus' teaching that was his personal creation. Since his disciples did not have the advantage of living in India and being immersed in the source of what he was teaching them, Jesus formulated various rituals to compensate for their not having access to the samskaras of Sanatana Dharma. These are what came to be called "Sacraments." Jesus formulated those rituals to empower his disciples' spiritual practice in the West. We use the sacramental rites that were formulated at the beginning of the twentieth century by Bishops James Ingall Wedgwood and Charles Webster Leadbeater for use by those who followed Sanatana Dharma and practiced Yoga in what became known as the Liberal Catholic Church.

Original Christianity

We use the term "original Christianity" because we want to get it across to those who read this book that Jesus' original teachings were those of Sanatana Dharma which he brought back with him from India. Our position is simply this: We cannot follow the teachings of Jesus outside of Sanatana Dharma because they are nothing but Sanatana Dharma. Jesus learned his wisdom from the sages of India and so must those who would follow him. Original Christianity also includes the practice of traditional Yoga as found in the Upanishads, Bhagavad Gita and the Yoga Sutras.

Paramhansa Yogananda

We are not the originators of this ideal. In 1920 Swami (later Paramhansa) Yogananda came to America to speak at a religious conference in Boston, Massachusetts. In his discourse at that conference he announced that he would be remaining in America and giving weekly classes of one and a half hours in length: the first half hour would be on the teachings of the Bhagavad Gita, the second on the teachings of the Gospels, and the third on the fundamental unity of the two. For thirty-two years he held to this approach. Today many people in East and West carry on that vision. We are just a few of them.

Paramhansa Yogananda was continually denounced by Christians as a Hindu missionary trying to fool Christians into converting to Hinduism, and denounced by Hindus as a Christian missionary trying to fool Hindus into converting to Christianity. He was, of course, simply presenting the truth. We are trying to do the same.

As Saint Thomas Christians we are definitely of Christ; and Christ is of India.

GLOSSARY

Acharya: Preceptor; teacher; spiritual teacher/guide; guru.

Atma(n): The individual spirit or Self that is one with Brahman. The true nature or identity.

Avatar(a): A Divine Incarnation.

Bhagavad Gita: "The Song of God." The sacred philosophical text often called "the Hindu Bible," part of the epic Mahabharata by Vyasa; the most popular sacred text in Hinduism.

Brahman: The Absolute Reality; the Truth proclaimed in the Upanishads; the Supreme Reality that is one and indivisible, infinite, and eternal; all-pervading, changeless Existence; Existence-knowledge-bliss Absolute (Satchidananda); Absolute Consciousness; it is not only all-powerful but all-power itself; not only all-knowing and blissful but all-knowledge and all-bliss itself.

Darshan: Literally "sight" or "seeing;" vision, literal and metaphysical; a system of philosophy (see Sad-darshanas).

Dharma: The righteous way of living, as enjoined by the sacred scriptures and the spiritually illumined; characteristics; law; lawfulness; virtue; righteousness; norm.

Gorakhnath: A master yogi of the Nath Yogi (Siddha Yogi) tradition. His dates are not positively known, but he seems to have lived for many centuries and travelled throughout all of India, Bhutan, Tibet, and Ladakh teaching philosophy and yoga.

Jiva: Individual spirit.

Karma: Karma, derived from the Sanskrit root kri, which means to act, do, or make, means any kind of action, including thought and feeling. It also means the effects of action. Karma is both action and reaction, the metaphysical equivalent of the principle: "For every action there is an equal and opposite reaction." "Whatsoever a man soweth, that shall he also reap" (Galatians 6:7). It is karma operating through the law of cause and effect that binds the jiva or the individual soul to the wheel of birth and death. There are three forms of karma: sanchita, agami, and prarabdha. Sanchita karma is the vast store of accumulated actions done in the past, the fruits of which have not yet been reaped. Agami karma is the action that will be done by the individual in the future. Prarabdha karma is the action that has begun to fructify, the fruit of which is being reaped in this life.

Maharishi: Maha-rishi–great sage.

Maya: The illusive power of Brahman; the veiling and the projecting power of the universe, the power of Cosmic Illusion. "The Measurer"–a reference to the two delusive "measures": Time and Space.

Moksha: Release; liberation; the term is particularly applied to the liberation from the bondage of karma and the wheel of birth and death; Absolute Experience.

Patanjali: A yogi of ancient India, the author of the Yoga Sutras.

Punarjanma: "Birth again;" rebirth/reincarnation.

Purusha: "Person" in the sense of a conscious spirit. Both God and the individual spirits are purushas, but God is the Adi (Original, Archetypal) Purusha, Parama (Highest) Purusha, and the Purushottama (Highest or Best of the Purushas).

Rishi: Sage; seer of the Truth.

Sad-darshanas: The six orthodox systems of Indian philosophy: Nyaya, Vaisheshika, Sankhya, Yoga, Mimamsa, and Vedanta.

Sampradaya: Tradition; philosophical school; literally: "handed-down instruction;" also a line of initiatic empowerment.

Samsara: Life through repeated births and deaths; the wheel of birth and death; the process of earthly life.

Samskara: A ritual that makes an impression or change in the individual for whom it is done. There are sixteen samskaras prescribed by the dharma shastras, beginning with conception (garbhadan) and concluding with the rite for the departed soul (antyshthi). The major ones besides these two are the birth rite (jatakarman), naming ceremony (namakaranam), the first eating of solid food (annaprasannam), the first cutting of the hair (chudakaraman), bestowal of the sacred thread and instruction in the Gayatri mantra (upanayanam), marriage (vivahanam), taking up of the retired life (vanaprastha), and taking up the monastic life (sannyasa). They are all done at points in the person's life when significant changes in the subtle energy bodies are going to take place. Thus the samskara protects and strengthens the individual at those times and also prepares him for those changes, making actual alterations in his subtle bodies. Although they are often made social occasions, they are very real instruments of change to facilitate and further the person's personal evolution. They are the linchpins of dharmic life, and essentially spiritual events.

Sanatana: Eternal; everlasting; ancient; primeval.

Sanatana Dharma: "The Eternal Religion," also known as "Arya Dharma," "the religion of those who strive upward [Aryas]." Hinduism.

Sanskrit: The language of the ancient sages of India and therefore of the Indian scriptures and yoga treatises.

Shankara: Shankaracharya; Adi (the first) Shankaracharya: The great reformer and re-establisher of Vedic Religion in India around 300 B.C. He is the unparalleled exponent of Advaita (Non-Dual) Vedanta. He also reformed the mode of monastic life and founded (or regenerated) the ancient Swami Order.

Shaiva/Shaivite: A worshipper of Shiva; pertaining to Shiva.

Shakta: A worshipper of Shakti, the Divine Feminine.

Shiva: A name of God meaning "One Who is all Bliss and the giver of happiness to all." Although classically applied to the Absolute Brahman, Shiva can also refer to God (Ishwara) in His aspect of Dissolver and Liberator (often mistakenly thought of as "destroyer").

Siddha: A perfected–liberated–being, an adept, a seer, a perfect yogi.

Upanishads: Books (of varying lengths) of the philosophical teachings of the ancient sages of India on the knowledge of Absolute Reality. The upanishads contain two major themes: (1) the individual self (atman) and the Supreme Self (Paramatman) are one in essence, and (2) the goal of life is the realization/manifestation of this unity, the realization of God (Brahman). There are eleven principal upanishads: Isha, Kena, Katha, Prashna, Mundaka, Mandukya, Taittiriya, Aitareya, Chandogya, Brihadaranyaka, and Shvetashvatara, all of which were commented on by Shankara, Ramanuja and Madhavacharya, thus setting the seal of authenticity on them.

Vaishnava: A devotee of Vishnu.

Vedas: The oldest scriptures of India, considered the oldest scriptures of the world, that were revealed in meditation to the Vedic Rishis (seers). Although in modern times there are said to be four Vedas (Rig, Sama, Yajur, and Atharva), in the upanishads only three are listed (Rig, Sama, and Yajur). In actuality, there is only one Veda: the Rig Veda. The Sama Veda is only a collection of Rig Veda hymns that are marked (pointed) for singing. The Yajur Veda is a small book giving directions on just one form of Vedic sacrifice. The Atharva Veda is only a collection of theurgical mantras to be recited for the cure of various afflictions or to be recited over the herbs to be taken as medicine for those afflictions.

Vishnu: "The all-pervading;" God as the Preserver.

Yoga: Literally, "joining" or "union" from the Sanskrit root yuj. Union with the Supreme Being, or any practice that makes for such union. Meditation that unites the individual spirit with God, the Supreme

Did you enjoy reading *The Christ of India*?

Thank you for taking the time to read *The Christ of India*. If you enjoyed it, please consider telling your friends or posting a short review at Amazon.com or the site of your choice.

Word of mouth is an author's best friend and much appreciated.

About the Author

Abbot George Burke (Swami Nirmalananda Giri) is the founder and director of the Light of the Spirit Monastery (Atma Jyoti Ashram) in Cedar Crest, New Mexico, USA.

In his many pilgrimages to India, he had the opportunity of meeting some of India's greatest spiritual figures, including Swami Sivananda of Rishikesh and Anandamayi Ma. During his first trip to India he was made a member of the ancient Swami Order by Swami Vidyananda Giri, a direct disciple of Paramhansa Yogananda, who had himself been given sannyas by the Shankaracharya of Puri, Jagadguru Bharati Krishna Tirtha.

In the United States he also encountered various Christian saints, including Saint John Maximovich of San Francisco and Saint Philaret Voznesensky of New York. He was ordained in the Liberal Catholic Church (International) to the priesthood on January 25, 1974, and consecrated a bishop on August 23, 1975.

For many years Abbot George has researched the identity of Jesus Christ and his teachings with India and Sanatana Dharma, including Yoga. It is his conclusion that Jesus lived in India for most of his life, and was a yogi and Sanatana Dharma missionary to the West. After his resurrection he returned to India and lived the rest of his life in the Himalayas.

He has written extensively on these and other topics, many of which are posted at OCOY.org.

More from Light of the Spirit Press

By Abbot George Burke (Swami Nirmalananda Giri)

May a Christian Believe in Reincarnation?

❧

Om Yoga Meditation: Its Theory and Practice

❧

The Gospel of Thomas for Awakening: A Commentary on Jesus' Sayings as Recorded by the Apostle Thomas

❧

A Brief Sanskrit Glossary: A Spiritual Student's Guide to Essential Sanskrit Terms

❧

The Dhammapada for Awakening: A Commentary on Buddha's Practical Wisdom

More of Abbot George Burke's writings can be found at the website of Light of the Spirit Monastery, OCOY.org.

You will find many articles on Original Christianity and Original Yoga, including *Esoteric Christian Beliefs*, and *Robe of Light*, a Christian cosmology. *The Word That is God* is an in-depth collection of citations from the scriptures and spiritual masters on Om. *How to Be a Yogi* is a practical guide for anyone seriously interested in living the Yoga Life.

And you will also discover many practical articles on leading an effective spiritual life, including *Foundations of Yoga* and *Spiritual*

Benefits of a Vegetarian Diet, as well as in-depth commentaries on these spiritual classics:

- the Bhagavad Gita,
- the Upanishads,
- the Tao Teh King
- the Aquarian Gospel of Jesus the Christ.

Recently added are a series of podcasts by Abbot George on meditation, the Yoga Life, and remarkable spiritual people he has met in India and elsewhere.

Sign up for our free newsletter and receive weekly blogposts, podcasts and newsletters with practical knowledge to improve your inner and outer spiritual life. Visit: http://ocoy.org/newsletter-registration

Visit OCOY.org today.